Paths THAT CROSS

Ps. 23:3

Betty Rich Hendon

Ambassador International
Greenville, South Carolina • Belfast, Northern Ireland

Paths That Cross
©2005 Betty Rich Hendon
All rights reserved
Printed in the United States of America

Cover design & page layout by A&E Media — Rita Blajeski

ISBN 1 932307 51 6
Published by the Ambassador Group

Ambassador Emerald International
427 Wade Hampton Blvd.
Greenville, SC 29609
USA
www.emeraldhouse.com

and

Ambassador Publications Ltd.
Providence House
Ardenlee Street
Belfast BT6 8QJ
Northern Ireland
www.ambassador-productions.com

The colophon is a trademark of Ambassador

Dedication

I dedicate this book to all my former students; you touched my life. Oh, how you touched my life! You also touched the strings of my heart and played music on it so rare and sweet. So, to all of you—every Judy, Carl, Curtis, Linda, Sandy, Tony—to every Billy, Robert, Joan, Nola, James—every Scott, Karen, Anna—every Peggy, Jane, Steve, Diane—to every one of you wherever you are now, I want you to know that you were unique.

You were a pathfinder to my heart, and I love you still. The classroom memories are still there. What a joy it was to be your teacher—to watch you as your knowledge expanded! You were a rare treasure in my memory bank, and I sincerely hope that I made learning a joy for you as I tried, in my own way, to be God's hand extended and to model his love.

Acknowledgements

To all of you over the years who asked me to pray for you, I am grateful. You have made me a better person. As I prayed for you, I received inner strength and peace.

To those of you who pray for me as I write, I am appreciative. Your prayers were my support line, because God heard your prayers.

To Billie Cash for your words over the telephone when I called you from Florida and shared the synopsis of my first ten chapters, "Why Betty, that's paths that cross, you stated in your excited manner. You must call the book *Paths That Cross*. That's what it is!"

I thank you for giving a title to my book.

To Opal Jackson, Ophelia Flowers, and Jan Thomson for modeling God's love in schools—for loving children as I love them—you are in my thoughts and prayers.

To my publisher, Dr. Samuel Lowry, I owe my appreciation and gratitude.

To my husband, Drexel, for his computer expertise and, to you the reader, I would like to express my heartfelt thanks. Without you I would not write.

Thank you all. I hope that some day our paths will cross.

Endorsements

Teachers have always played an important role in the upbringing and education of our children. In these days their role is even more critical, as children face a myriad of distractions, many of which are negative, both at home and away. We, as parents and citizens, depend on dedicated teachers to provide a positive environment to influence our young ones. Betty Hendon is such an educator.

In *Paths That Cross*, Betty Hendon shares her personal journey in a story full of love, hope, expectation, encouragement, excitement and inspiration. She taught me 12th grade English at Memphis Technical High School many years ago, and I still have fond memories of a young teacher with a sense of excitement and wisdom beyond her years. She had a knack for challenging students at all levels, and in a friendly and compassionate way. Her writing conveys that trait strongly.

Paths That Cross will provide inspiration for people of all generations. It is easy to tell that Betty Hendon writes with sincerity and that she gives us a glimpse of what it is like to lead a God-centered life. I believe that her words will help many to have a close walk with their Lord.

—Roland N. Pittman, Ph. D.
Professor of Physiology, Virginia Commonwealth University

"Reflecting on my reading of Chapter Seven of *Paths That Cross*, I find one phrase that resonates louder than all the rest—"give me the courage to move my feet." In her discussion of walking with God, Betty Rich Hendon cautions that we can have the clear direction, but we have to "step out" with God in the lead. Over and over again in *Paths That Cross*, Betty illustrates stepping out in courage."

—JUDY CHATHAM
Author of *A Whirlwind's Breath* and *The Amber Necklace*

"How blessed I feel to have crossed paths with Betty Rich Hendon! She is someone who truly radiates God's love in everything she does—and her writing reflects that. She lives what she writes and she does it with a fresh and enthusiastic manner. Her ability to see people through God's eyes comes out through all the interesting situations and events she encounters along the path of life. Her latest book is a must-read for all of us who wish to grow in our faith walk and all its winding paths."

—KATHY KAVELMAN MARTIN
Free-lance Writer/Owner of Kathy Martin Communications
Collierville, TN

"Betty's book provides great insight and clarity about the need for each of us to be sensitive to the leading of the Holy Spirit in our daily life's. It further endorses the fact all of us can and will be used by the Holy Spirit. The leading of the Holy Spirit is not limited to a select number."

—RANDY DIGIROLAMO
Senior Manager at FedEx Express

Table of Contents

	Prologue	ix
1	Paths of Faith	1
2	A Bitter Path	9
3	A Blind Path	15
4	Road to the Cemetery	19
5	Pathway of Names and Nicknames	23
6	Pathway to Our Hearts	29
7	Paths That Cross	37
8	Path to the Cross	47
9	Guides Along the Path	51
10	One Path God Made Just for You	59
11	Pathway to Peace	69
12	Pathway to Friendships	77
13	Path to Protection	89
14	Dark Paths	93
15	A Winding Path through the Iris	103
16	Roadblocks	107

17	Pathfinder	115
18	Paths of Evil or Paths of Promise	125
19	Paths before Them	133
20	Wisdom's Path	141
21	Guarding the Path of Minerals	147
22	Parallel Paths that Never Cross	155
23	A Serpentine Path	165
24	Guideposts on the Path	171
25	An Unwelcome Path	177
	About the Author	181
	Bible Translations	182
	Endnotes	183

Prologue

During my life, I have walked down many paths—some by myself—others with a group.

No two paths were alike. Each had its unique trees, flowers, waterfalls, green grass, or pebbles, sand, and rocks.

At times, I needed to be alone—alone with God.

Alone with time to think and pray.

Alone to solve and deal with problems.

Just ALONE.

At others times, I needed companionship.

I remember the times that I traveled from Tennessee to Florida with my mother. At first the road around Montgomery, Alabama, was a two-lane highway with all its intersections. Later, the large interstates with as many as six lanes came into existence.

With changes came speed. More people came in and out of my life.

As the paths changed, so did my life experiences.

I met people in airports that I shall never see again. One person that I'll never see again was at Wal-Mart in Florida. I will never forget that young man. You made a keen impression on me that day with your words, "It's too late for me."

They echoed in my brain. They still echo and bounce back to this very day, and as you read my book, you will see yourself in chapter seven.

I am glad that our paths crossed that day. Chris, you were the impetus that I needed to write this book, and I thank you.

1

Paths of Faith

The day had arrived.

The picture frame had to be repainted.

Every time that I moved my floral picture, I had to spray the frame a new color. The yellow frame that looked great hanging over the pecan guest bed clashed with the colors in my bathroom.

The color of the frame could be painted white. That would blend well with the other colors. I already had some spray paint. Now, all I had to do was tape the glass inside the frame with masking tape.

The task was tackled with great enthusiasm. I was eager for a decorating change, and my inspiration came the day that my son returned from a trip and presented me with the tapestry from Venice, Italy.

The guest bedroom would be the perfect place to display it, and I was thrilled with the scene of canals, gondolas, and colorful buildings on the water. The gondolier would be in full view for me to see it as I walked down the hall to the master bedroom.

At the age of eleven, God had painted my young heart a different color. Where it had been yellow with anger, greed, and other eleven-year-old vices, he took his paint brush and covered me in pure snow white, and when his canvas was complete, he covered me in love and placed me on an easel for others to view.

I did not know that day where he planned to hang his new work of art or that his portrait would be viewed by thousands of students. Without realizing it, nine years later I would have my teaching certificate from Vanderbilt University and students would view my life from every angle in the classroom.

This was the path that was charted that hot September day for eleven-year-old Betty Rich.

Barry had been so pleased when I opened my gift.

He knew my taste—any tapestry that had a water scene would appeal to his mother.

He had faith that it would please me. It did. I was thrilled and excited.

I thought of a young man in the Bible who had faith.

Daniel as a young man had extraordinary faith—his faith was tested to the ultimate limits.

Faith, the focus of Ephesians 6:16, is portrayed by Daniel when his king asks him to explain the meaning of his dream. Daniel requested a little time before giving King Nebuchadnezzar a response to his dream—the dream that had become a nightmare to the ruler.

Chapter two in the book of Daniel depicts exactly what happened and how Daniel handled the situation with great wisdom for one so young.

Daniel knew exactly what to do. **PRAY.**

He also knew to enlist the help of other prayer warriors.

We all need friends to pray when a crisis comes in our lives. Asking people to pray for my needs comes hard for me; I don't want to bother people who are busy. But, I must not think like this. I have discovered that I receive the greatest blessings when I pray for others.

It is all right to ask other people to pray, and I am still working on this weakness of trying to carry the load myself.

Wayne, my husband's brother, was stationed in the Philippines. One night, when he and his wife Johnnie were sleeping, a gecko dropped from the curtains on their bed. It landed on Johnnie, who was terrified by the ugly creature. She jumped out of bed yelling and screaming.

Sometimes in our daily routine, a gecko drops out of the sky, and we are faced with an ugly crisis.

This is what happened to Daniel that day; a period of crisis clothed him like a robe and pierced his heart like a dagger. His very life was in danger.

What did he do?

Daniel asked his prayer partners to pray, and God answered their prayers by revealing to Daniel that same night in a vision the secret which saved their lives.

I can imagine the anguish in his mind when he heard that the king had ordered all the wise men of Babylon executed when they could not decipher the meaning of his dream.

Many others had failed. Would God give him the meaning of this dream that was so unsettling to the king?

Daniel's heart had been stabbed by word from the king, and he knew that this was a time for prayer.

This should have a meaning for you and me in this current age.

There is a time for individual prayer in our lives, but there is also a time for uniting with others in joint fellowship and prayer

Joint prayers bombarded heaven for Daniel's request. God answered.

When God revealed the meaning to Daniel what did he do?

In return for the answer, Daniel did not fail to give God thanks.

He thanked God for revealing to him the knowledge necessary so that he would continue to live and to serve God as he grew older.

So many times when I have prayers answered, I remember that I have not given God the proper thanks. As soon as the thought flashes into my mind, I immediately stop and tell God how grateful I am for his blessing.

I tease my sister a lot by telling her that she is short on faith, and she usually nods her head in agreement. The one thing that she is not short on is prayer. She has a bountiful prayer life, and if I need to go to the throne of God in prayer about a request, I call Verlene and ask her to pray.

I can depend on her prayers.

The last time that I called her with an important request, we were over 9,000 miles apart, but the distance made no difference.

Verlene's response was so precious, "Do I have to pray right this minute, or can I wait until I read my Bible right before I go to sleep? I always pray after I read my Bible," she stated so sincerely.

Laughingly I assured that my request could wait thirty more minutes until she was ready for bed and had read her Bible.

I am not sure that you have a sister who is a prayer warrior like mine, but isn't it wonderful that individually we can take any gecko that falls on us at any time of day to our creator and he hears them if we belong to his family.

I am thankful that God placed the two of us in the same Rich family—I am indeed blessed in two ways by being born a Rich and by becoming daily more and more "rich in Christ."

The later is the most important as we view the news each night and hear about the precautions that we should take and the survival kit that we should stock and have on ready in case of a chemical, nuclear, or biological attack.

We need faith like Daniel's faith for our tomorrows. He was just as human as we are. If he could have this faith spoken of in the Old Testament, we can have the same faith now.

We need faith that our creator knows and understands what is needed for this day and age.

In Memphis, by the mighty Mississippi River, stands a pyramid. A sports arena which glistens like silver as you view the direct sun's reflection from an airplane. Years ago, the city viewed it as a great project; today it is a liability to the city government. On the local news, we were informed how much money it could cost to keep it open and how much to close it—about $500,000 a month even if we closed it, I believe the reporter quoted.

At the time that officials voted to build the massive pyramid, it generated great controversy. The project soon won approval. Officials prioritized the funds.

Without realizing, at times we place our priorities in the wrong order. For some people, the pyramid is built in this order:

WHERE ARE CHURCH AND GOD?

For some reason our list of priorities is confused, because we have left out the more important aspect of our lives—the aspect of having ETERNAL LIFE.

What steps should we take in our survival kit of life?

The first step is to stop kidding ourselves into thinking that everything is all right if we just do not think about it.

Terrorism will go away if we don't turn on the news and listen.

Just go fishing.

Go to a movie and get our minds off of depressing news.

More steps are needed.

We must make the first step which is THINKING—clear thinking about the seriousness of the seventy years that we have promised.

These 70 years apply to some—others die much younger.

Recently, I read in the local paper that a .38-caliber slug hit a former Miss Memphis as she walked her Doberman. The bullet, from the gun of an angry father, was meant for his daughter's boyfriend. The dog owner had walked into the path of the bullet without knowing that she was in the middle of a domestic dispute.

What about us? Are we occasionally in the middle of danger without realizing it?

The second step is to admit that we need help; we need God's help.

This is hard for a man or woman in our society to do. We are geared to being self sufficient. Do it ourselves is our motto. Don't ask anyone for help is the way that we have been trained, and it is hard to break the mold and become as clay in the potter's hand. Our pride stands in the way just as it stood in the way of the rich man in the Bible that asked God what he should do to be saved.

God hit him at the top of his pyramid when He told him to sell all he had. Why, he couldn't do that so he went away sad.

He also went away UNSAVED. Eternal life costs entirely too much money, and he was unwilling to make the trade.

What is standing in your way for step two?

Possibly, you continue pushing the thought to the back burner of your mind. Like Scarlet in *Gone With The Wind*, you will think about that tomorrow.

Do you have the power to assure yourself that you will drive home tonight and arrive there safely? Can you control all the circumstances between your job and your home? If not, who does? The person who does have control of the oceans, the stars, the winds, and the rain is exactly the one who has control of the number of years that you will live.

This is the person that you need to be on a first-name basis with—not that important person in your organization who controls promotions—although that is important to each of us. We all have goals and aspirations. We all have plans for the future.

We all want to chart our own paths, but are we following God's time table?

Do not procrastinate so long that you never get around to taking step one and step two.

There is a given time to get on the right path—the path of righteousness!

The Holy Spirit must be striving with our hearts for us to be able to be united into this family of faith, and the Spirit will not always touch the human heart. Many people will reject Christ and their hearts will become harder and harder. They will even think in their minds that they are just fine as they are.

How sad it is to meet people like this on the path of life.

My heart goes out to each, and I want to wrap my arms around them and pray for me. God loves them more.

Time with the Master

What path are you on at present?

- Searching for a better job?
- Trying to make more money?
- Working to buy a new car?
- Just making enough to place food on the table?
- Saving for a new home?
- Spending all extra monies on fashionable clothes and shoes?
- Putting money in the bank to buy a new boat? To take a cruise? To go on a summer vacation? To buy a new business? To buy your dream recreational vehicle?

There is nothing wrong with ambition. All of the above are noble—just consider His will as you make your priorities.

• Do you have a void in your heart even after you meet a certain goal?

• Could this void or emptiness mean that you need to ask Christ to forgive you for pursuing your own goals, not His, and to allow Him to direct your path?

DO THIS TODAY BY PRAYING WITH ME THE FOLLOWING PRAYER:

Lord, I need help with the direction that my life is taking at this time? Please forgive me and help me to see clearly the next step that I should take. Allow me to be the Christian that you desire me to be. Amen.

2

A Bitter Path

This hazy path was not fully lighted, but instead it was an inchoate path that winded through the pasture where cows grazed in the hot summer sun. Scattered between the green meadows, like they had been broadcast by a farmer, were pedaled flowers with a yellow center. They were not ordinary flowers like a housewife would place in a vase; instead they were greatly disliked despite their beauty.

They were bitter weeds.

Sometimes life is like that—a beautiful green pasture sprinkled with bitter weeds that entice the cows in the meadow to eat their fill. Life seems to be full of green meadows, but as we enjoy the pleasures, we get a spoonful of bitterness, and like a cow which lunched on these bitter flowers in the pasture, we pass on our bitterness to our children and our associates at work.

Until I was nine years old, my parents owned a cow. The city limits ended about five houses west of our house, a white, two-storied frame building with seven acres, a peach orchard and a barn in the back. Therefore, we could have chickens and a cow.

My mother could even milk a cow. I tried one time at the age of seven without any luck, so I gave up. As child, I instantly knew the taste of milk when a cow had been grazing on bitter weeds and refused to drink it.

It tasted awful!

There are times in our lives when we come in contact with people who have been grazing in the pasture of the world, Satan's world of dark lights, forbidden sex, prostitution, alcohol, cursing, gambling, and pornography. Before some people finish one statement, our ears are flooded with the sounds of curse words, slurs, and loud laughter.

My heart is grieved when I hear profanity and God's name taken in vain; if I feel pain, how much more so must Jesus, who gave his very life for those who use profanity, ache for the sins of mankind.

There are others bitter weeds that we must avoid like smallpox, or measles. One of these is jealousy, which has a healthy appetite. The more food you give it, the more it craves.

It can quickly grow from a petite form to a ghastly shape. The neighbor buys a new boat; a colleague is promoted on the job when we know that we deserve to be promoted above this individual. A friend of ours gets a new RV with all the bells and whistles. An acquaintance buys a new mink coat, and another marries a millionaire after her husband dies.

On and on the monster grows like an ameba—larger and larger as we eat our morsel of bitterness.

I must admit that I have to guard my own heart in this area.

Nobody is exempt from having thoughts of jealousy.

Another bitter weed called greed raises its ugly head; greed is a hard taskmaster, who has an enormous appetite. In marriage, we MUST keep the score even. Everything must be 50-50, so when our husband buys a new truck, we go shopping for a new bedroom suite that we know we deserve. We max out our credit cards in a fit of anger.

If he can buy something, so can we. The bills pile up and the bitterness grows until it explodes. Quarrels over charge accounts develop on a weekly basis, and we go to bed at night angry—angry at our mates, or just angry at life in general.

This bitter weed leaves an awful taste in our mouths that nothing seems to rinse out. New clothes do not satisfy.

We are no longer happy with our family life and we seek outside happiness. The name of this bitter weed is extra-marital satisfaction, because if he can have what he wants, so can we—two can plays this game. We convince ourselves that all is fair in this game of life. We will do whatever it takes to get his attention without thinking that this bitter weed may be too hard for one of the mates to swallow.

One cannot forgive.

The bitter weed of pride is a monster to chew and digest. It rolls around on the tongue and creates a ghastly bitter taste. No one should have to swallow that pungent and acetic taste. It is tart indeed! The spouse detests it with a full measure of PRIDE—it is slimy like stewed okra—slimy, green, and unappealing to the pallet, so the spouse refuses it and obtains a divorce to save face.

What started this circle of bitter weeds?

Where will it end?

Are there children involved in the marriage?

If so, the children are placed in the middle, and the spouse moves to another state to avoid child support. On the few occasions that the children are contacted by telephone, he confront the ex-wife and the children are upset as they hear the loud voices of the two people that they love the most. Their emotions are ripped apart. Children think that they are the cause. He does not love us or he would stay.

They cannot reason as an adult. They are too young.

Bitter are the vices of sin.

The once satisfying, rewarding and sweet forbidden fruit has become harsh indeed.

Eve found this out in the Garden of Eden when she was given the curse of childbirth and great pain.

Adam discovered it in Genesis when he labored to raise his food and to cultivate the fields.

Today, our society discovers that the forbidden fruit has worms inside.

Time with the Master

- What does our textbook, the Bible, teach about forbidden fruit? (Proverbs 13:2)

- What does it say about jealousy and pride? (Proverbs 13:10)

- What does the Bible instruct us to do regarding mistakes in marriage? (Proverbs 17:9, TLB)

- What does the master teacher say about pride? (Proverbs 29:23)

- Do we have Biblical principles on the subject of lust? (II Samuel 11 and 12)

3

A Blind Path

> Afoot and light-hearted I take to the open road,
> Healthy, free, the world before me,
> The long brown path before me leading wherever I choose.
>
> —WALT WHITMAN[1]

Poetry with its sweeping rhythm, its meter and beat, has always spoken volumes to my heart. I breathe it into the gates of my heart.

It makes me sad.

It cheers me.

It encourages and challenges me.

I know an individual who has never seen a path.

She has never seen a star, the moon or a field of red clover. The ocean cannot be imagined by this individual.

The sky is only a figment of her imagination. The mighty Mississippi near her home is only as she depicts it in her mind. She has never seen a mountain, a babbling brook, or a raindrop.

A unique—even auspicious—aurora covers this member of the Severson family, Betty Ann. I met her for the first time in the 1960's. She was raised by Norwegian parents on a large farm in South Dakota. She had many siblings, but she also had a handicap.

Betty Ann was blinded at birth when a doctor in a rural community picked up the wrong bottle and dropped a few drops of acid into her eyes. Her parents held her while the procedure occurred even though she screamed and cried. An honest mistake had taken place that had a profound effect on her life.

Betty had a talent.

Betty was given a gift—a lovely voice and an ear for music.

Betty learned to play the piano and the organ. These lessons filled her lonely moments during the day. After receiving her high school diploma, she attended college in S. Dakota; later she was accepted by the Julliard School of Music in New York, where she received voice lessons to complement her ability to play the organ and piano.

She was on the Ted Mack Amateur Hour on television one year. She also sang for Lion's Club Conventions and for her local church.

Along with this, she taught students in a school for the blind.

Betty decided to take training to travel independently at the School for the Blind in Little Rock, Arkansas.

This path led her to meet her future husband, who was blind.

These two young people became interested in each other and eventually grew to love each other and were married in Nashville, Tennessee.

Years later, two sighted children were added to the family—a boy and then a girl. Betty diapered them, made formulas to feed them, cooked and cleaned the house, and labeled each can of food in Braille so that she could read what was stored in each can from the grocery store. At this time, her husband worked at a local health club in Sioux City, Iowa, and no relatives lived in that state.

Many other people are blind. We well remember the man who was led down flights of stairs by a seeing-eye dog in the World Trade Center Twin Towers when terrorist drove airplanes into the two buildings as we stared in shock.

They never see the sunset. She will never see a rainbow—never know what colors look like.

She made a statement to me one day that I shall never forget. Let me share her words with you:

"I wish I could see what my children look like, but I know that the first face that I shall see will be the face of JESUS. This makes me happy."

Many times I heard her sing her favorite song, The Lord's Prayer, but the words she spoke to me that day will never be forgotten.

Although Betty has no eyes, the eyes of the Lord are on her guiding her path every day.

"I will guide thee with mine eye."[2]

This daughter, wife, mother was a rock for her family. She sang in her church choir for years as she sang and witnessed for Jesus. She has lighted the path for her children and grandchildren to follow.

By her songs of praise, she has lighted the path to salvation for those who listened to her music and her personal testimony.

I am pleased that our paths crossed.

I am honored to be in the same family, because you see she is married to my husband's brother.

We are both in the Hendon family and in the family of God. We both share the same name—Betty Hendon.

Time with the Master

- What member of your family has been a blessing to you personally?

- Have you told that person?

- What person has crossed your path this month that had an impact on your life?

- How could you walk on a path of godliness so that you will have an influence on someone in your family?

4

Road to the Cemetery

Some individuals just seem to possess a querulous disposition while others display a happy nature on this leisurely promenade of life. At present, the time frame for the average person to live is approximately seventy to eighty years.

My brother who had a love for sports, politics, and people ended his trip in fifty-one years, which is a short span of life in my view.

My grandfather traveled through the horse and buggy days to the decade of airplanes by achieving a span that bridged about ninety-three years. From the age of fifty-two, he lived daily with pain as his companion, but he learned to cope by taking two aspirins every four hours. Pain never chained his spirit or his loving disposition.

But time marched on and he too took his ride in a gray coffin to the Neill Cemetery—our family cemetery.

Time will march on and death will wrap his arms around each of us.

It plays no game of favorites.

Death comes to all.

My son Barry mowed the lawn for a dear couple who were in their late eighties. Mr. St. John took his ride first, and his wife moved to Waco, Texas, to be near her son. Barry kept in touch with her by sending her cards and by sending her oranges from Florida.

On January 13, 1987, she wrote this letter to him:

Dear Barry,

I know that you had a nice holiday with your parents—hope that they stayed a few days with you.

We are enjoying our lotion to keep us beautiful.

My son and I went out to see a retirement home. It's new, in fact not finished but I think it is too expensive for me although my son says not. This includes utilities, transportation, emergency call system, planned activities, once-a-week maid cleaning, three meals a day, laundry, security twenty-four hours, professionally trained medical personnel, and if you need it, help dressing or bathing. They will monitor your medicine.

1 bedroom apartment 850 sq. ft
$1,050 a month...extra person $150 more

2 bedroom apartment, 2 baths 1150 sq. ft.
$1550 a month...extra person $150 more

Residential Suites: Efficiency 450 sq. ft.
$1470 leased monthly...extra person $30 more

If you just want one meal a day, subtract $100 from the leasing cost. The meals, if you don't want meals included, are $4 a meal.

I would have to take care of sister too—she has a saving but that's to take care of necessities and for burial, etc.

Enclosed is an article out of Waco paper. I thought you might be interested in.

Take care of yourself and have a nice New Year.

Love,
Mrs. St. John

What a lady she was!

At this time Mr. St. John was in her nineties but she was still so full of spunk. Every time she returned to Memphis to visit Mr. St. John's grave she would call me, and how I enjoyed her calls! She was an inspiration to me. She was still so sharp with her keen sense of humor, but as you can see from her letter—she was planning for the time in her life when she would need to take the road to a retirement home.

This elderly woman was wisely concerned about her future.

At every stage in life, we should be concerned about our future and think about the path we are following each day.

Are we giving our employer an honest day's work?

Do we listen to the advice of our superiors on the job?

"Listen to this wise advice; follow it closely, for it will do you good, and you will pass it on to others: TRUST IN THE LORD."[1]

These words of wisdom from the Bible are affable to any age, but as we grow nearer and nearer the age of retirement and the stage of our life when we may need assisted living, it is safe to trust in the LORD.

If you are still young, consider these two verses:

"True humility and respect for the Lord lead a man to riches, honor and long life."[2]

"If you must choose, take a good name rather than great riches; for to be held in loving esteem is better than silver and gold."[3]

Our best manual for raising a child is still the Bible:

"Teach a child to choose the right path, and when he is older he will remain upon it."[4]

Time with the Master

- Are you a young married person with children?

- When should you start training your children if you desire them to take the right paths in life?

- What is your responsibility?

- What outside help will you need?

- What family support can you depend upon on a daily basis?

PRAY WITH ME:

Loving God, help me to be the mate that I need to be. Also, help me to train my children by example by taking them to church instead of sending them. I praise your holy name. Amen

5

Pathway of Names and Nicknames

As a teenager and as a young adult, I strongly sensed that I did not have time to be putt-putting my way through each day. I knew that my path was being guided by a gentle, loving God whom I desired to please.

Today as the memories are flashing like ethereal pictures in the sterile air, I can hear my parents' peals of laughter echoing down through time—gay thrills of sounds which produce warm-hued emotions and feeling, and I am proud to have had them as my parents.

I am proud to trace my ancestral path: Rich, Solomon, Gray, Young, Neill, Poole, Wood, Diffy, and Hafley.

Some of these paths take me to England—others to Germany—still others to Ireland. My mother's goal in life led me on a path to the Holy Land.

I am a product of them all.

I have the Rich Roman nose. My sister has the Young freckles. My cousin has the Young red hair. My brother had the Solomon hair line. On and on we can go tracing the ancestral path to resemblance and to country locations.

We are all a product of our inheritance.

I inherited a love for children from my father, and a love for travel from my grandfather Solomon. I cannot move fast enough to get away from memories of them or from their influence on my life.

Genes can be a blessing or a curse. My cousin inherited crippling arthritis from Papa Solomon. When this condition hit him around the age of fifty, he considered it a curse. It certainly caused him to die much younger than other cousins.

Names are very important to us. New parents-to-be take hours and hours pondering over the name that they will give their children.

Names were also important to God.

God changed Abram's name to Abraham. God asked him to leave his people and said that He would guide him and bless him, and Abram built an altar—not to glorify himself but to recognize God's visit to him.

I can imagine his thoughts as I read the twelfth chapter of Genesis.

I am comfortable around my people in this land. I do not like unknown paths, but I must follow God's path.

Abram must have had thoughts similar to this, but I surmise that the real clincher was the fact that he would be a blessing to generations to follow him on this pathway of life.

We read in I Chronicles 4:9-10 about a mother who chose an odd name for her son. Jabez's name meant "distress," but he called on the Lord and asked God to please be with him.

What a difference these words made in his life!

That was certainly an odd name, but his mother said that she bore her child in distress—so she named him by this name.

Names and Nicknames

Names are very important. A person's name is important to all of us. My husband has a pet peeve—he dislikes for anyone to mispell his name. We receive mail a lot spelled Herndon, Henderson, or Hendron.

The same applies to telephone calls. A sure give-a-way that an individual does not personally know my husband is for them to call him Mr. Drextel or Mr. Dexter.

I am sure that is why we chose a simple name for our son—a name that no one mistakes or misspells.

Names are so important that fund raisers using names is popular.

We received a letter from Nashville, Tennessee, explaining that we could purchase a brick with our name on it and that it would be placed commemorating Tennessee's 200 years of statehood—Bicentennial Celebration on the Bicentennial Capitol Mall.

Path of Volunteers

This Path of Volunteers is the central walkway to a permanent monument marking a milestone in the history of our state.

We purchased a brick with our son's name inscribed on it, because our son's name was important to us.

In my hometown, Savannah, Tennessee, names inscribed on bricks were used as a pathway in the "Trail of Tears" to the Tennessee River.

A letter was mailed to me by one of my alma maters regarding a path—a Campus Pathway.

The University of Memphis also followed suit with their promotion to build a legacy of names one brick at a time in the new Student Plaza.

Names in the Bible were so important that the victorious king could rename the losing king.

Because I wanted to know the origin and meaning of my name, I purchased a book called *The Name Book* which contains more that 10,000 names with meanings.

I hurriedly turned to page 153 to see what my middle name, Joyce, meant—its origin and spiritual significance.

The Bible verse under Joyce quotes Ps. 16:11.

"You will show me the path of life; in Your presence is fullness of joy, at your right hand are pleasures."[1]

This flooded me with pleasure and joy as I read. I was thrilled that my sister had chosen Joyce when Mother asked her if she wanted to choose my middle name when I was born.

My brother who was ten years older had chosen my first name—Betty, a derivative of Elizabeth, a Hebrew name that has a spiritual connotation of consecration.[2]

This gives me a feeling of assurance and comfort.

I am blessed by both names.

My brother and sister did well.

You know that the person who creates something usually names his creation. Also the person who paints a picture usually signs his name at the bottom of the picture.

Yes, names are very important to us.

In Genesis 10:25 we read that Peleg's name means division, because in his day the earth was divided.

Mankind all spoke one common language until they decided to follow the path of self glory and built a monument to themselves—the tower of Babel.

God had other paths for them to take. So, He changed their language in order that they could no longer communicate with each other; therefore, the monument for self glory was left incomplete.

I wonder if God is displeased with us today when we place so much importance on our names in a way to give glory to ourselves!

We place our names on buildings—on the entrances to bridges—and the list goes on.

Yes, our names are important to us.

Names and Nicknames

My uncle gave his relatives a path of nicknames.

This uncle never called me by my name.

Uncle Otis always called me Boots.

He left an unusual legacy behind him when he died. Otis never had any children of his own but you could tell he loved and enjoyed children.

He gave every young relative a nickname. While I was Boots, my sister was Zippy. He said that she was always zipping around so fast that he could not catch her.

Could I have reminded him of a pair of boots?

I never asked him why I was Boots—I just accepted his nickname and signed my letters from college that way.

This nickname was Otis's legacy of love.

He always called our names with a twinkle of love in his eyes and with a smile a mile wide across his face. He made us feel special with the affection, warmth, and genuine love that radiated from him—there was no doubt about it—we felt good.

Otis Rich built his pathway of nicknames in his unique way that lasted long after his tragic death in an accident on the highway which wasn't his fault. Sometimes this is how life is—without warning on this path of life our lives can be changed. Lives can end—that is a reality.

More children will be born in the Rich family but none will receive a nickname from Otis. I was one of the fortunate ones.

Time with the Master

- How do you react when someone calls you a bad name?

- What example do you give to others listening?

- Would God be pleased with your reaction?

- If not, how can you make a change?

- What help do you need in making this change?

- When will it take place?

PRAY THIS PRAYER WITH ME:

Master, I desire to follow your paths more closely. Help me to guard my mouth and my thoughts so that my actions will be a role model for my loved ones and friends. In the loving name of Jesus, Amen.

6

Pathway to Our Hearts

God speaks in different ways to individuals.

The Lord spoke to Paul one night in a vision and told him not to be afraid because he was with him.[1]

On other occasions, he spoke directly to people as he did to Mary and Martha when their brother died.[2]

"Betty, God speaks to you a lot in dreams, doesn't He," were the words softly spoken by my lifelong friend, Becky.

I pondered her words and agreed.

Many times, He does speak to me during the night in dreams, but I do not find this to be strange—just unique.

I treasure these occasions.

During the night hours, I seem to tune in and listen more closely. I enjoy all forms of communication. At night, I am more pliable—more willing to listen, I guess.

My mind soared back to July, 1982, to a dream about two ladies from Iraq. Somehow, I knew what country they were from in my dream.

The two women in long white robes and white headdresses with a black band covering with foreheads appeared before me. Both had dark complexions and were very short.

When they saw me, they drew closer together and began conversing in a low whisper using their native language.

Without hesitation, I began conversing with them in the same language.

For about thirty minutes, I shared with them the plan of salvation, stories about Jesus, and many Biblical truths.

They just stood still in front of me and listened attentively and quietly absorbing each story from the Bible that I related to them.

When I awoke, I was totally exhausted and spent—fatigued.

I was so exhausted that I had to take a nap to rest from the dream, which weighed heavy on my heart—so much so that I recorded every detail and placed my writing in a secure place.

I somehow knew that this dream would be important to me in the future.

In April of 2003, God reminded me again of this dream.

"Do you remember that dream about the two ladies from Iraq?" He said to my mind.

"Why, yes," I responded. "Is that why I have been so burdened about the people of Iraq?" I questioned.

At this period of time, each day's news reported on events in Iraq, and a desire to have a book translated into Arabic had been placed on my heart. The burden was so deep that I cried when I thought or spoke to anyone about it.

My heart was touched by God. I knew that I had been given another task that I had to complete. I just did not have the expertise to accomplish the task at hand.

Here again, I guess that I would just have to step out by faith and see if I could find someone with knowledge of the Arabic language.

I have asked my prayer partners to start praying that this book translated in the Arabic language would find its way to people living between the Tigris and Euphrates rivers. Who knows what the mighty hand of God can bring to pass! I have found from past experience that when God places a task on our heart, He will stand by us until it is completed.

In 1982, He had asked me to do something for him that was not completed until 2003, but it was completed.

Twenty years in his time frame may be like a day in our human minds. Since He is omnipotent and loving, there are times that we must trust his timing. His timing is perfect.

Notice the task that one mother was given to save her baby boy.

This mother went to great effort and definitely followed a unique path to protect her newborn. Her son should have been killed at birth, because the king of Egypt commanded the midwives to kill all male babies at birth.

These midwives feared God more than the king; therefore, they spared the male babies.

This mother hid her beautiful baby at home for three months and when she could no longer do so, she devised a plan.

She followed the path to the river's edge and gathered papyrus reeds in order to make a little boat or basket. Then she covered it with tar to waterproof the basket. She went to great lengths to secure the basket for her son.

When it was complete and was waterproof, she placed her child in the basket and carried it to the river. She was well aware that the daughter of Pharaoh came each day with her ladies to bath herself in the river.

Pharaoh's daughter heard the baby's cries and saw what a well developed child he was.[3]

Their paths crossed.

This mother's plan worked because it was also the plan of God for Moses. God had a plan for Moses to lead the children by a long and winding path through the wilderness for forty years.

What a God we serve!

Moses' mother was even paid to nurse her own child while he was young.

What a turn of events for her!

Her baby was safe and was raised in the king's palace with every comfort known at that time.

"And when we obey him, every path he guides us on is fragrant with his loving kindness and his truth."[4]

As God had a plan for the life of Moses, today in our decade, he has a plan for your life.

Yes, you are that important to God.

But don't take my word for it. Let's see what the person who made you has to say when he responded to the prophet Jeremiah.

Jeremiah communicated with his God.

"O Lord, I know it is not within the power of man to map his life and plan his course—so you correct me, Lord; but please be gentle."[5]

God stated this to encourage him; it should encourage you.

"For I know the plans I have for you, says the Lord. They are plans for good and not for evil, to give you a future and a hope. In those days when you pray, I will listen. You will find me when you seek me, if you look for me in earnest."[6]

Do not be too upset when God redirects the path you are taking at present. Let me illustrate by my own experience.

I was already teaching school when my husband started searching for a position. He received a lead from a hospital in Marion, Indiana, for which he was trained.

No opening existed in Memphis at the time.

We traveled by car to Marion and Drexel went for the job interview. I also went for an interview to teach English. We were both offered a position, so we went house hunting.

We discovered a homey older home with a fireplace with white built-in bookcases on each side and nice hardwood floors. This particular house appealed to us.

Everything was on go—we took my contract home to sign and return.

It was summer so we had time before school started to move our furniture and adjust to a new area and a new routine.

Our path seemed to be leading us out of state.

Just as soon as we returned to Memphis, Drexel received a call for an individual at the hospital. In their conversation this individual stated that he would like to sell his house in Memphis and work in Florida.

We were elated that we had found a home in Memphis and a position also. Our path had changed. God had redirected our plans and we were able to remain within a hundred miles of both sets of parents.

We were near as our parents aged—two battled cancer and two struggled with a stroke and heart problems.

God knew that my husband would be working in the hospital where my brother would battle for his life for fifteen months.

God knew the future.

God gently led us to make the correct decision relating to employment. He knew the path which we needed to chart, and Indiana was not on his road map.

Our path is not always this clear—sometimes it reminds me of driving in the rain when it is hard to see a mile down the road, or to hitting a patch of fog when we really have to slow down to thirty miles an hour.

When these times come, and they will, we know that the fog will not last forever and the rain will stop eventually and the sun will shine.

When I was very young—age four, five, and six—my dad worked in the woods clearing a path in the woods by cutting tall trees and transporting them to a sawmill.

Loggers know the importance of clearing a path for the truck to travel in order to haul the timber to the mill so that it can become paper after the proper processing. Are we leaving a well-marked path for people to follow who are not Christians? If they live as we live will they be able to find Jesus?

At times, the roads in the woods are merely muddy trails leading up and down rolling hillsides. These trails lead back to gravel roads and finally to paved roads. Of course, the paved roads are well marked and easier to follow.

Life is like that.

At times we are traveling on muddy roads—we do not see clearly why we must enter the hospital for surgery, or why our investments on the stock market keep going down and our savings are going down with them.

We want clear answers. Clear answers don't always come.

We are confused. Still we know that our sovereign God is in control. He knows where we are headed even though the path is vague and just thinking about our circumstances is overwhelming.

Time with the Master

- Are there times that Jesus speaks to your mind or spirit during the quiet night hours?

- What task has He placed upon your heart to do?

- Do you spend time in prayer covering this task in prayer?

- Are you standing too far away to hear his still, quiet voice? Are you afraid of what you might be required to do? Please don't be; Jesus never demands more that he equips us to do.

- Is the path too foggy to see?

- Do you appear to be wandering in the dark?

PRAY THIS PRAYER WITH ME TODAY:

Heavenly Father, help me to have the desire to listen to your voice when you speak to my mind. Equip me to do the task that you place upon my heart. Guard me from the day-to-day things that would hinder me from hearing your voice and from completing what you want me to do. I shall trust you and your timing. Amen.

7

Paths That Cross

Over my bed in the master bedroom, I have a picture of a peaceful winding path—a scene that is so pleasing to the eye that it calms me by just viewing the path shaded by tall trees and surrounded by beautiful, blooming flowers in their vibrant colors of red, rose, and soft purples against the lust green foliage.

God created the trees and the flowers, but I was glad that some artist labored to capture that peaceful scene.

Each spring these flowers bloom and give glory to their creator. Nature sings out praises. How can we miss the message of his love? Are we too busy to see?

I took time one sunny day to sit on the bench in front of Wal-Mart and to wait for my husband.

It was just another ordinary day.

The sun was shining and warm. I had made my purchases and was content to rest and wait, but what followed was unexpected. We never know what path our life will follow on any given day.

This December day started as a routine day—I ate my hot oats with butter and sugar—went to Wal-Mart for paper plates, napkins, tissue, and deodorant—just those necessary items. Another routine day.

My husband and I have two-way communicators that I call walkie-talkies; we carry them when we are in large stores shopping. We can each go our own way and notify each other when we finish shopping.

I stood in line, paid the cashier for my items and walked outside to wait. I parked myself on the bench in front of Wal-Mart to wait for my husband who had remained with our car.

I reached for my bright yellow walkie-talkie that I had attached to my waist when a clean-cut young man with a cigarette between his lips walked by.

I'll never know why I spoke to him. Maybe it was the fact that he reminded me of my son.

This young man who appeared to be college age noticed my walkie-talkie and commented, "That's a good idea. Your husband must be inside shopping."

"No, actually he's outside; I was the one inside shopping."

To my amazement, I heard myself continue the conversation in a manner that surprised me, "You look to be about the same age as my son, and as an old school teacher, I'll tell you the same thing that I would tell my son. You'd stay healthier if you would stop smoking."

He removed the cigarette from his lips and stated as a matter of fact, "I'm twenty-seven and it's too late for me."

With a deep sadness in his voice, he continued, "I already have cancer. It is lymphoma, but it has nothing to do with my lungs. I've started my treatments."

He paused by me to continue smoking when I felt compelled to ask, "What is your first name?"

"Chris."

"Chris, I wished that I could have taught you. I bet you were a good student."

I shared with him that I had worked with young people all my life as a high school and college teacher and as an elementary principal. He told me about two trips that he had taken to the principal's office in elementary school. He was bored in class and got himself in trouble.

"Chris, would it be all right with you if I prayed for you?" (I had in mind to remember him in my nightly prayer time.)

"Sure," he replied eagerly and immediately bowed his head.

Seeing that he thought that I meant right there in front of the store, I still wanted to be certain

"Would it embarrass you if I prayed right now?"

"Embarrass me, for someone to pray for me. No way!" he said emphatically.

So, right there on the concrete walkway in front of a busy Wal-Mart, I sent up a prayer for Chris, a receptive twenty-seven-year-old without any hair on his head. His treatment had left him bald.

This certainly was not the path that I had planned for myself that day. I am not usually that bold with a stranger. I am more reserved, but for some reason that day I think that God was leading me. God knew that I was willing to be used and those words—it's too late for me; I already have cancer—pierced my heart.

I saw a young man that God had created in His image who was hurting. I do not think that I will ever forget what I heard myself saying as I prayed for Chris that day.

"Lord, we worship you as our Creator. You are the God of our universe, and you are worthy of praise. You created Chris and knew him by name even before he was formed in his mother's womb. For every Bible verse that Chris reads, will you remove cancer cells from his body? We thank you for the answer to this prayer this day. In the wonderful and holy name of Jesus, Amen"

My ride came and I left him that day knowing that I shall never cross his path again in this lifetime, but I have faith that we will some day walk and talk together on streets of gold laughing about my yellow walkie-talkie and our meeting in front of Wal-Mart.

We never know who is hurting and when a prayer is needed.

Looks can be so deceiving. We can have our Shakespearean acting face plastered on to show the world when deep inside we are hurting.

That is the precious thing about the Holy Spirit. It can make us sensitive to the needs of others.

There is a time to cry with others. There is a time to laugh with others.

That day God knew that he needed a prayer.

It is both rewarding and exciting to follow his path—it leads to so many precious people, and I have found that often their brave exterior conceals a hidden world of turmoil and pain.

It is great to know that our God is ubiquitous, existing everywhere at the same time. He is omnipresent, loving, and caring—not wanting a single one of us to die without accepting Jesus as our savior.

I certainly hope that those of us who are his children can make a conscious effort to be courteous, kind, and gentle to those who cross our path each day.

Walking with God is the most exciting thing that I can do.

I walk a path each day to the mailbox to thumb through the junk mail and to separate it from the bills. Even though I enjoy receiving letters in the mail, this path to the mailbox isn't nearly as exciting as the paths when God is leading us at the most routine times.

I met my husband for lunch two weeks ago—we had decided on Patrick's because of their delicious vegetables and chicken rice soup. After this we could not resist the dessert menu—my favorite part of the meal. I ordered chess pie and Drexel ordered sweet potato pie.

Since we were in separate cars, I thought that I would look through the Williams Sonoma Store; it was only a few doors north on this particular strip mall. Between these stores was an Oriental rug store, and for some unknown reason I drifted inside and viewed vibrant Persian rugs of every color and hue.

A salesman came forward. After discussing his rug selection, we talked of other things. The young sales clerk was from Armenia; he proudly showed me his billfold size picture of his two small children. I have no idea how our conversation led to both of us having a strong belief in God, or how it led to his asking me to pray that he would find a new profession. I prayed a short prayer on the spot, and when I finished, he placed his business card in my hand and wrote his name on back as a reminder to me to continue to pray.

I assured him I would pray for his job for the next seven day.

How could I forget his pleading eyes!

A new profession was very important on his list of hierarchy for that particular time in his life.

"I will instruct you (says the Lord) and guide you along the best pathway for your life; I will advise you and watch your progress."[1]

These words encourage me when I wonder which decision I should make with the different choices we face on a daily basis. Some choices are large; others are small—like what program to watch on television.

On one given night, I had these television movies to choose from: *The Truth About Jane*, a mother tries to cope with her daughter's lesbianism; *The Next Best Thing*, a yoga teacher and her gay soul mate have a child together; and *The Final Conflict*, Damien the Antichrist becomes an adviser to the president.

Choices make us who we are. As the computer specialist says, "Garbage in, garbage out."

It is even truer with our character and our well being.

I have prayed many times this prayer:

"Hallelujah, heavenly father! I am your child, and you are indeed my father who knows what course of action that I should take. Open the right doors for me to enter and close and lock the doors that I should not walk through. Place a floodlight on the next step that I should take and give me the courage to move my feet.

I thank you for the answer to this prayer. You are faithful to hear my prayers. Amen"

Then I remind myself of those verses written by David in the book of Psalms—How thankful I am that his words were written for me to read this day in the USA!

What if the book of Psalms had not been written?

I could not have memorized the 23rd Psalm in the third grade.

The words in that chapter are just as applicable today as they were when David who had been a shepherd boy told us not to stand in the "path of sinners"[2] and "the Lord watches over all the plans and paths of godly men, but the paths of the godless lead to doom."[3]

Another verse penned by David encourages me when I become impatient for an answer to a situation.

"Don't be impatient for the Lord to act! Keep traveling steadily along his pathway and in due season he will honor you with every blessing."[4]

On television recently, I heard a daughter read a letter that she had written about her mother who was a correctional officer at a prison. This mother had struggled to raise her family by herself, and it was not easy to pay all the bills.

I was impressed by these words spoken by her daughter about how fortunate people were to come in contact with her mother who had such a big heart. This was the way her daughter phrased it—"anyone lucky enough to have crossed your path."[5]

Paths that Cross

This mother responded by saying that her friends were more valuable than any diamond that could be bought.

No wonder her daughter wanted to praise her!

My heart sends up a thank-you prayer:

Heavenly Father, I thank you for giving me a godly mother who loved to read the Bible and whose heart was tender to God.

I also thank you for allowing the Holy Spirit to draw me to you and I thank you for forgiving my sins as a child of eleven. I thank you for hearing my prayers and for answering prayers that are in your will. I desire to live a life that is pleasing to you. I also thank you for placing me in the Rich family as well as the family of God. Amen.

Time with the Master

- Can you look back at a time in your life that your path crossed that of a stranger that you helped in some way?

    You may have made a phone call for someone with a flat tire sitting on the side of the road, or you may have taken time to change their tire or to air up the flat.
    You may have given a word of encouragement to a stranger at the funeral of a friend.

- Are you living the type of life that you would want your family or your child to duplicate?

- If not, what is one thing that you can change?

- Whose life are you following?

- What will you do if that person disappoints you?

- Rejects you?

- Are you strong enough as a Christian to continue following the path that Jesus leads you to take?

PRAY THIS PRAYER WITH ME:

Lord lead me in the path of righteousness. Keep me secure and sheltered under your wings. Carry me across the rough spots and keep my heart in tune so that I can hear your still, quiet voice when you speak to my heart. Amen.

8

PATH TO THE CROSS

Verlene and I went on a summer vacation to two pretty southern cities. Our childhood friends, Marietta and Becky, went with us. A great deal of pleasure came from viewing the well-landscaped gardens in Charleston, South Carolina, and in Savannah, Georgia. Versatility in colors pleased us as we viewed waterfalls and ponds incorporated into sections of the gardens along the path.

All of the blossoms were worth noticing but my thoughts zeroed in on the lily pads—in my mind lilies were equated with God's purity and holiness.

As I walked with my sister down the well-planned garden path with its variegated, sun-dappled plants placed beside the brick sidewalks, my mind was drawn to thoughts of Jesus' path to the cross—a winding one without pleasure—he appeared to be a pawn in the hands of evil men, but was this true, or was God really in control?

As Jesus walked in the Garden of Gethsemane with his disciples, the group of men probably talked about the events of the day—as he instructed them and gave the guidance that they would need in the future.

We now have years of reading and dissecting Biblical truths, but the disciples faced new territory and they needed Jesus' calm words of assurance as they walked with him in the garden.

They would be experiencing this particular scenario for the first time on a day that seemed to be a normal one with birds soaring above the olive trees, but soon a weed of anger and greed would choke out the sweet smelling scent of flowers.

As this greed enlarged in Judas' heart, a woodpecker drummed on a nearby trunk and a hawk soared above the scene—just a normal day, but soon their world would be topsy-turvy.

The book of John details the events of their time, and the climate of that day and age. Jesus gave us instruction about three things:

- He knew God's timing.
- He knew God's plan.
- He knew Death would follow.

As I walked the path to Gethsemane and stood where I could view the old city of Jerusalem, my heart sensed the heartbreak that our Savior must have felt.

Tears formed in my eyes and ran down my cheeks. I could not stop them, because I knew that I was walking along the same path that he had taken with his disciples.

I thought of some words from the Bible; Oh Jerusalem, Jerusalem, how often would I have taken you into my arms, but you wouldn't let me.

I seemed to share his heartache and pain on that day—a day I shall never forget.

His path took him to the Mount of Olives.

His path took him to the temple to teach.

"I am the Light of the world. So if you follow me, you won't be stumbling through the darkness, for living light will flood your path."[1]

Then, there is Jesus' PATH TO PILATE[2], the governor, who saw no crime because He was Galilean. He sent him to King Herod.[3]

The PATH TO HEROD followed where the soldiers mocked him and placed a robe on him, Herod sent him back to Pilate[4].

Next in line was a PATH BACK TO PILATE.

A PATH TO CALVARY[5] took place afterwards.

The PATH TO A SEPULCHRE[6] was His next trip.

The people at that period in history did not understand who He was, just as people today do not understand how God is directing them.

Many times we see God's hand leading us in hindsight.

And, there is nothing wrong with that. We are human with all of our personality quirks and our character flaws.

I often pray for God to use floodlights to show me the path He wants me to take—a flashlight is not bright enough for me to see clearly his directions.

I must say it is easier since I start my day just breathing in Jesus by quoting scriptures of praise followed by prayer and end my day the same way. Like the keys on a piano, it keeps me in tune.

"Since the Lord is directing our steps, why try to understand everything that happens along the way?"[7]

That same question is pertinent in the age that we live.

Time with the Master

- Do you feel sometimes that you are a yo-yo on a string going up and down without a plan for you life?

- How can Jesus' path to the cross change your life?

IF YOU WOULD LIKE, PLEASE PRAY ALONG WITH ME.

Dear Jesus, please give me a plan for my life. Help my to study your word and to search for meaning for my life. I truly desire to please and serve you. Please help me and make me a strong Christian. Help me follow Christ to the cross and to accept what he did—knowing that it will change my life. Amen.

9

GUIDES ALONG THE PATH

Visiting the British Museum was quite an experience! I had previously viewed the Hope Diamond and Westminster Abbey. I reflected on this tour without a guide. I had only one day to spend in the museum, and I wanted to see everything.

We certainly miss a lot of information when we do not have trained guides as we visit tourist locations.

God places tour guides at strategic stations on our path through life.

The name of our first guide was introduced in Proverbs 11:3 which states "A good man is guided by his honesty."

Honesty was a handsome and friendly fellow who broadcast instructions and who gave clear, concise directions guiding us on the first segment of our tour.

Honesty has many faces. In most events, his opponent dishonesty tries to win the race for our attention (and really for our very souls). He covers himself with beautiful garments—a vest of cheating—cheating on a test at school—taking small items home from work—cheating on our spouse.

A contemporary of mine, also a school principal, paid for a school computer with school monies, returned the computer, and spent the refund on personal items instead of returning the funds to the school account.

This individual received attention, but in the wrong way; she lost her position and brought shame to her family. Cheating can be coordinated with many costumes, but in the end it can have serious consequences. CEO's of major companies like Enron, IBM, WorldCom, have had their problems in recent years. Changing the figures in the books to make the company more attractive so that more people will purchase stock is a form of cheating.

Recently, more and more people are getting caught at the little game they are playing.

They followed the wrong tour guide through their path up the corporate ladder.

Honesty is a character trait that can be developed at a young age. We teach honesty to our children by example—example teaches better than words.

Dishonesty is shrewd—he dresses in a suit of green dollar bills by subtly telling the real estate salesman to make a deal by sliding a little under the table. "…man is destroyed by his dishonesty."[1]

What is done in secret usually comes to light, and it is best not to follow this guide.

Our second guide on this museum tour of life was Integrity, a well-trained director who gave us a choice of plugging in the earphones and listening to principles of living a life full of justice, or just taking the fast track by skipping the audio tape made by a professional commentator.

Other companions and I chose striking out on our own.

By choosing the later, we missed a lot of educational truths and made many wrong turns and twists, but we thought we could find our own way through the corridors—anyway we were in a hurry so we went from corridor to corridor until we found a room marked with a big black sign—SELFISHNESS.

I already knew most of the items in this room, because I had used them daily. The decision was made to skip this exhibit.

The next one was labeled STUBBORNNESS over the door.

We did not want to miss that one, because we felt a kindred spirit. Perhaps, you were in the room with me, but I personally didn't recognize you among the hundreds who were milling around laughing and slapping each other on the back.

This Stubbornness room seems to attract a lot of individuals.

No use lingering here too long; I knew this information as a child.

The next hallway led to a room labeled simply READING ROOM, which looked enticing until I spied an open book in the center of the room. Upon further inspection, I found this book had the title, BIBLE.

I wanted no part of this room, I didn't have time in my busy schedule to take time for reading that book—besides, a book with the same title was on a table at home just catching dust. I must remember to dust it off when it was convenient for me. I believe I may have dusted it last month.

The same applied to the fourth room marked PRAYER. Clearly lighted in a showcase was a vase with an engraved sign telling people to drop a prayer request in the vase and people would pray for each request.

I was too private a person to acknowledge that I had a need, so I just sloughed that off, shrugged my shoulders, lifted my chin, and marched on.

I had no time in my tour for reading religious literature or for prayer. Who did they think I was—a religious fanatic? I was doing just fine by myself. I didn't need anyone praying for me.

Oh, I forgot to introduce myself; my name is IMA ANNA HURRI.

I want to get everything out of life that I can, but I don't want to be bothered, or help anyone else along the way.

Just get out of my way and let me pass on in this museum of life. I might miss out on something important so don't stand in my way.

But wait, this maze through this museum is more complex than I first thought!

Where did I make the wrong turn? Somewhere on this fast track I had lost my companion, Integrity. Now that I needed him, he was nowhere to be found. Let's face it. I am lost.

Lost!

No, as I turned around I spied my second companion, Impatience.

Good! At least I am not totally alone.

Although we had skipped many of the essentials for healthy living, we still pushed on through the open doors of the museum.

The exit sign was near, but we did not want to leave right now. We were too young to take the room with the door marked clearly GRAVEYARD.

We wanted to push on in life—have more fun—see more sights along the way. Try more thrills. Do more dangerous experiments. JUST LIVE LIFE TO ITS FULLEST!

With GRAVEYARD so near, I somehow felt a strong urge to locate my first companion, INTEGRITY.

I breathed a short one-word prayer, "HELP!" I also yelled out his name, because I was beginning to be frightened.

"INTEGRITY" I shouted in my loudest cheerleader's voice.

"Where are you? Do you hear me?"

When I was ready to give up and take the exit, Integrity heard me, reached out, touched me on the shoulder, and took my hand.

"It's time for a lunch break," Integrity informed the group, "and I have asked my friend, RIGHTEOUSNESS to join us if that is okay with you?" His voice was so calmly reassuring that I immediately agreed. Something that I would not have done a few hours before, but somehow I had changed.

RIGHTEOUSNESS when I first viewed him looked much too severe to suit my untrained eyes. I bet he never has any fun, but when I heard his soothing, melodic voice, I found myself drawn to his warm strength of character. I had never been around anyone who reminded me so much of the sincere warmth of my mother's voice as she gently wiped my childish tears.

He slowly explained to me that I really needed two more friends to help me on this museum path—CHARACTER and GOODNESS.

I found myself agreeing and was quite shocked at myself. I really must have changed since I saw that shortcut that I could have taken through the exit marked GRAVEYARD.

Character impressed me with his patience and kindness. My previous friends—stubbornness, greed, and dishonesty—had little of these characteristics. Character was even as well equipped as Integrity, so I followed—but at a distance. They might be too holy for my likes.

Character stated quite clearly, "The next section of your journey demands your complete attention, because Goodness is very soft-spoken and mild in manners. You have to listen attentivly as he speaks to your heart as well as your ears."

He handed us a brochure with the following written on the outside cover: Proverbs 11:6 LB and Proverbs 14:22 LB. As I turned to the inside of the pamphlet, I found detailed explanations regarding these two verses that I was totally unfamiliar with.

I was beginning to learn more and more about this path through the museum of life.

Really, I could not think of a more reliable guide than

Goodness, because I found that I liked him quite well in fact. He seemed more loyal than Stubbornness and Selfishness.

Character told me that Goodness had just received an award which the whole city celebrated and which caused Goodness to be very happy. Also, he had a good rapport with his superior and often asked for advice and worked hard at his job to become a better guide.

I was impressed with his credentials.

Goodness informed me, "I will allow my assistant, KNOWLEDGE, to take over now; he has been in training for three months and has passed the test to lead you on to the next floor.

I had met Knowledge in elementary school and had been his friend until the sixth grade when I found I had little time for his friendship. IMA ANNA HURRI was in too big of a hurry to learn much in that grade in school but how to pester the other students.

I looked down at my brochure and read these words printed in bold type: "…through knowledge shall the just be delivered." Proverbs 11:9

What did that mean?

Knowledge must have read my mind, because she explained all aspects of the brochure before guiding me to the next section of the museum and turned me over to KINDNESS, who had a delightful personality—quite charming with that infectious grin that ran like an upside down rainbow across his face.

He must have read my mind too because he said, "You must be hungry by now. You have been on this trail for hours. Would you like to eat?"

When I responded in the affirmative, he took me to a break room and gave me a liberal portion of Proverbs 11:17 LB. This nourishment tasted so good that I wondered why I had refused this type of food when I was a younger student.

My mother had coached me many times to eat liberally

from this vegetable, but to no avail because I wanted to hurry and play with my friend, Stubbornness.

Kindness had been a big help to me and I was surprised to hear my voice say, "Thank you very much. I really was hungrier than I thought. You have nourished my soul, and I am indeed appreciative."

My, I must be changing to take time to say that, I thought to myself.

At the end of the day, I had gained a lot of insight that I should have slowed down and heeded before. But, you know me, I was in a hurry.

I also sensed in some strange way that I was different and that these tour guides had head me in a direction of discovering God's will for my life so that when I arrived at that final section marked GRAVEYARD and took Death's cold hand, I would be ready to follow him without guilt

- without regret
- without blame
- without fear

I was prepared now because somewhere along the tour, I had cried out to God for help and had received Salvation as my closest friend—a friend so close that he seemed to live inside my heart. I could trust him with life and death.

But before that happens I told myself that I must take time to read that Bible that once belonged to my mother.

Ima Anna Hurri had a total regeneration—a new way of thinking!

Ima Anna Hurri had total peace.

Time with the Master

- Could you see yourself in this chapter?

- Have you been in too big a hurry rushing from one appointment to another—from one assignment to another to take time to listen to KNOWLEDGE, GOODNESS, INTEGRITY, CHARACTER, and RIGHTEOUSNESS?

- If so, will you slow down and find time in your busy schedule to listen to God when He speaks to your heart?

Then, surely Goodness and Mercy
will follow you all the days of your life. Psalm 23:6

10

ONE PATH GOD MADE JUST FOR YOU

How can one gardenia with its intoxicating, fragrant perfume bring so much pleasure?

These were the words unspoken in my mind as I viewed my two gardenia bushes from the bedroom window, as the sunlight riding across the water eliminated the shadows on the canal behind my house and heralded the beginning of a new day.

Later that same day, the bright Florida sun would hammer my head as I walked in the path. As I stood looking from the window, my mind went whirling back to a time when I was seven years old and stood on the wide eight-foot front porch in Savannah, Tennessee.

For weeks I had begged Mother, "Can I go barefooted now?"

"No, not until the buttercups bloom."

"Oh, please let me; p-p-l-l-l-e-e-a-z-z-a-a," I cajoled.

Like a child, I thought that if I coaxed her sweetly, she would relent.

Not my strong-willed mother. She stayed firm and as tall as her five-foot three-inch frame would allow, "When it is warm enough for the buttercups to bloom, then you can go barefooted in the front yard."

To go barefooted for the first time in the spring was the height of pleasure.

So, for weeks I waited and watched those green stalks as they formed buds that would gradually spring into yellow flowers. Then my toes would be released from my shoes. They would be free to wiggle to their hearts content.

This waiting was hard for a seven-year-old girl who needed to feel the soft green blades of grass under her toes.

I waited weeks.

I waited days.

Finally, the waiting was over.

I saw yellow buttercups, but somehow the anticipation surpassed the joy. Summer had arrived. I wiggled my toes. I walked down the path between the buttercups to the mailbox that stood across Highway 64. Little did I know that I would live to see my childhood home with its buttercups replaced with an asphalt drive through for a bank, or that the house would be torn down and replaced with a lumber company.

But the mind is magic—I can be that little girl again. I can travel back through the years and become that child with long, dark brown hair and eyes that matched.

I could trace that path back in my brain like a computer path and see how God was guiding me as a young child when I attended prayer meetings that were conducted in homes. If Mother went, I went.

One Path for You

I always thought that I was closer to Mother than her other two children because I came along last—ten years after my brother and five years after my sister.

I had that special distinction of being called "THE BABY."

"Is that your baby, Zelma?" acquaintances would ask my mother.

"Yes, this is Betty Joyce."

Many people in my childhood crossed my path—influenced my development. From my grandfather, Papa Solomon, I learned how to love family. From my mother I learned how to love God and family stories. From my father I learned how to love life, adventure, sports, and children; and from my grandmother how to love Florida beaches, sand, and water.

I also received from the Solomons the trait of tenacity and stubbornness. This has been a double-edged sword in my life.

No individual knows the turns and twists our path will take on any given day, but like an astronaut we must prepare ourselves for life—we go to school—we get on-the-job training. An astronaut practices the same routine over and over preparing for the day of LIFT OFF.

We need to cover ourselves in the complete space suit that we need when we prepare to operate this space shuttle of life. We should purpose in our mind to develop this habit:

1. I will be truthful with people today.
2. I will stay calm at work and not argue with coworkers.
3. Today, I will do what is right. I will treat my peers as I would want to be treated even if it takes a lot of effort.
4. I will be honest and give an honest day's work for my pay.

By practicing, we are placing part of our space suit on. You will find that it really fits well because God made it to our exact measurements. Just take one day at a time and God will assist you in your daily routine on your job or in your home. He will remind you of your desire to be honest in your dealings with others.

We know that we cannot succeed alone, but neither could the astronauts train and go into space alone. We have seen on television the myriad of workers seated at computers assuring their success on a mission.

We can read about the help we need in Ephesians 6:14-17.

These words stand out:

- Truth
- Righteousness
- Gospel Of Peace
- Faith
- Word Of God
- Salvation
- Prayer

These are our space suit to protect us from the enemy of our soul, SATAN.

We are astronauts for Christ. In His branch of service, we do not fight against people we can see. We do not see Satan; therefore, we have to fight him using the weapons listed above.

"For the weapons of our warfare are not carnal, but mighty through God to the pulling down of strong holds;"[1]

"I use God's mighty weapons, not those made by men, to knock down the devil's strongholds. These weapons can break down every proud argument against God and every wall that can be built to keep men from finding him. With these weapons I can capture rebels and bring them back to God, and change them into men whose hearts' desire is obedience to Christ."[2]

Our space suits aren't really that burdensome and heavy. God tailor makes each one to our exact size, and the task that He requires of us is perfectly suited to our personality, our ability, and our liking. Did he not make us? Does he not know our likes and dislikes? Does he not love us beyond all human love?

By practicing the seven above, we are taking on the righteousness of Christ—we are being Christ-like in our daily activities. This "armor of righteousness"[3] covers us with those intangibles that the eye cannot see.

The covering of:

- Love
- Tenderness
- Kindness
- Forgiveness
- Rapport
- Gentleness
- Mercy

You can sense and feel these qualities but you cannot see them. They are the eternal foundation of our pathway to heaven. Love is like sand—the soft grains we feel under our feet as we walk barefooted in the sand on the beach. It is gentle and touches the heart.

"For I am the Lord your God, the Lord of Hosts, who dried a path for you right through the sea, between the roaring waves."[4]

Love is a blanket covering our faults.

God loves us just like we are. Our flaws will not cause his love to cease for as long as we live. This love that He has for you is so great that nothing can separate you from his unending, bountiful love.

But don't take my word for this—let's see what the Bible has to say. "For I am persuaded, that neither death, nor life, nor angels, nor principalities, nor powers, nor things present, nor things to come, nor height, nor depth, nor any other creature, shall be able to separate us from the love of God, which is in Christ Jesus our Lord."[5]

No path travels so high that He is not there. Take the train to the top of the Swiss Alps. He is there.

No place in the ocean is so deep that His love is not there. Travel the continents. He is there.

- He is omnipotent.
- He is omnipresent.
- He is the everlasting Father.
- He is Jehovah.
- He is the Prince of Peace.
- He is Abba Father.
- He is all in all.
- He is the Counselor—the Mighty God.
- He is King of Kings.
- He is Lord of Lords.
- He is our Shepherd.
- He is Alpha.
- He is Omega.
- He is omniscient.

Our existence on earth may end, but He is unending, unchanging, and the light on our path. If you know him, this light shines through you. You one day will be as He is. You will take on all the attributes of the Father.

"But this precious treasure—this light and power that now shine with us—is held in a perishable container, that is, in our weak bodies. Everyone can see that the glorious power within must be from God and is not our own."[6]

You cannot get away from his love for his love is:

- Eternal,
- Boundless,
- Incomprehensible,
- Beyond Measure.

And as his child, you will inherit, all of his traits of righteousness. As we look into his face, we will take on his character.

One Path for You

Yes, even his forgiveness.

Last week as I exercised in the workout room in Florida, I had a conversation with an older man that really touched my heart. He said that he had not spoken with his brother in five years and did not plan to ever speak to him again.

It was connected with the settlement of his mother's estate. I shared my heart with him and asked him to please forgive his brother for the hurt he had caused him. I explained that he would have such peace that he would wonder why he had not done this before.

Life is too short for such hurt and pain. We have to learn how to forgive. Our nature is to move on and forget that person. We don't need them in our lives, but the sad thing is that we are hurt by this action as much as the other person.

It is possible to learn how to forgive.

The attribute, tenderness, is felt—not seen. It is the gentle touch of a mother's hand wiping the tears from her baby's eyes. It is the touch of wiping away the gravel from the toddler's skinned knee.

Tenderness heals the soul. Kindness and tenderness are knitted together in the same fabric by the thread of love.

You will find that you cannot hold grudges against those professional people who have stabbed you in the back climbing the corporate ladder of success. This can cause ulcers.

Forgiveness is the dew that cleans your soul of impurities. God does not send all the dew on earth in one day, but every morning a little dew is on the grass. The ability to forgive comes a little at a time and waters our heart with gentle love from God, and as He holds us in his arms, we are able to walk over the rough pathways of life and to forgive.

Just as we know the heat of the deserts of Arizona, He knows the heat and stress that we face on the job. He knows the pressures and the emotional stress as time limits and deadlines plague our daily schedule. A report is due by 4:00 p.m.—a floral design must get to the funeral home before the funeral—on and on the deadlines fly by.

He knows the sound barriers that boom in our ears, the constant ringing of the telephone at work, the ringing of the cell phone in our car, the constant demands on our time, and the never- ending lists of jobs to complete.

He knows!

He cares!

"Don't worry about anything; instead, pray about everything; tell God your needs and don't forget to thank him for his answers. If you do this you will experience God's peace, which is far more wonderful than the human mind can understand. His peace will keep your thoughts and your hearts quiet and at rest as you trust in Christ Jesus."[7]

What have we to fear when he covers us with his "feathers"?[8]

In God's right hand is POWER and MIGHT.

What have we to fear if his right hand of power and might is on our side? "Both riches and honour come of thee, and thou reignest over all; and in thine hand it is to make great, and to give strength unto all."[9]

Isn't it amazing how many answers to our daily problems are covered in the Bible!

Perhaps this translation is easier to understand: "Riches and honor come from you alone, and you are the Ruler of all mankind; your hand controls power and might, and it is at your discretion that men are made great and given strength."[10]

We are given the strength that we need when our path is so rough and steep that we need extra strength to carry on our day to day activities.

I have personally found that he gives us an extra covering and extra strength when there is a death in my family. The memories of his help never cease to amaze me.

Finding faith is the path to life.

I had make the wonderful discovery that life really is a journey on the path through the decades of our lives and not a guided tour through a museum; that the people (some I shall never meet in person) who touched my life by writing books, poetry, essays, biographies, magazine articles, autobiographies, and newspaper articles were a part of my growth and development.

The path is not always an easy path to follow, but it is a rewarding one; take my friends Ramon and Wanda. God's path for them led them on a meandering journey to many foreign countries where they have been an instrument in the hand of God and a voice in the wilderness. Like John the Baptist preparing a way for Jesus to enter the hearts of unbelievers.

Ramon's prayer life as a young youth leader at church was what set him apart from other young men his age. I watched him as he disciplined himself to give time each day for prayer—discipline is required, because many worthwhile activities vie for our time, energy, and attention. I'm thankful he crossed my path.

Ramon's prayer life was constant.

Although I was older, he was an example for me to follow. I prayed that I could be as focused. As Ramon, I knew that the path where the Shepherd leads us is the best trail to follow, and I realized that the good shepherd would be at my side and would only use his staff if I was in danger.

Time with the Master

- Is there a family member that you need to forgive?

- Is there a friend or co-worker that you need to set things right with today?

- Can you find the courage (oh yes, it takes courage) to talk with this person and tell them that you forgive them?

- Do you need extra help with the pressures on your job?

- Do you know how to pray?

IF YOUR PRAYER LIFE IS RUSTY, READ AND PRAY THIS PRAYER WITH ME.

Jesus, give me a forgiving heart, and also give me the courage to tell others that I forgive them before it is too late. Make me a stronger Christian so that I can be an example to my family. I thank you for your love for me and I trust you today to show me the right path to follow with my life. Amen.

11

PATHWAY TO PEACE

Although the Civil War was a blood bath for both the North and the South, Robert E. Lee's voice after his surrender was "one of the greatest forces for calming the feelings that the war had aroused both in the North and the South."[1]

After the war was over, Lee was offered the presidency of Washington College—this man who was graduated second in his class of 46 at West Point; he accepted, and after his death, the college was renamed Washington and Lee University.[2]

This Virginia native who had followed a path to war now followed the path to education and to peace by being a role model and by obeying the laws. By his actions, he became a good citizen within the United States. He could have chosen to leave the country and to establish a "government-in-exile,"[3] but instead this West Point graduate chose a different path—a path to peace.

Maybe your personality is confrontational and you seem to stir up and agitate people. You even have fun doing this. You like to keep things lively.

Maybe you are not a leader like General Robert E. Lee. You are merely a follower and you seem to be following the wrong path.

Where is this path leading you?

Do you have inner peace?

How do you find inner peace?

This path to peace does not apply to world peace; it does not apply or refer to peaceful existence between two countries. This path has always been littered with obstacles—a tree down here and a bridge washed out there, so to speak.

Your personal path to peace may not be brightly lighted; the road signs may not be clearly marked. You may sense that your life is spiraling out of control like you are driving a car toward a bridge that a barge had hit. A section is gone and you are speeding full speed ahead to drive over into the black darkness of waters that used to be blue and friendly during the day but are now murky and back—the sky and the water form one dark entity.

This path that you are on gives you no inner peace.

The path to peace that I refer to isn't the peaceful coexistence of employees in a large corporation. It isn't even the unity of a family unit.

Instead, the path to peace that I am talking about is that inner peace of mind when you wake up at night and cannot sleep. You find that you want it but you have not been able to find it to date. You sense that others have it while you flounder around like a seagull swooping down to the water to catch a fish to eat.

You are still just flapping your wings with no success.

Your soul is hungry for something you cannot place in words.

Some of us, like the seagull, search for peace in the pursuit of wealth. We work hard. We are not like the man who commented that a man should work only half of the day—it did not matter if it was the first twelve hours or the last twelve hours. In his humor, he made his point that a man must be committed to achieve his goal.

Others of us search for peace in the form of purchasing objects—obtaining the largest art collection, owning the largest house on the block, or having three homes at the same time.

Maybe you are searching by being the best player on the soccer team, or by being the bully of the fifth grade.

None of these paths will fill the void in your life and give you total inner peace.

We try to buy our children all the toys that we did not receive, or all the pretty clothes that our parents could not buy for us, because they were working hard to stay ahead of the creditors. Our children may be the best-dressed teenagers at school, but this will still not fill the longing in our soul for true peace.

Or, fame may be our pursuit for true happiness and peace. To see our name in lights is our major goal. We practice hours on end to be superior at tennis, golf, swimming, boxing, singing, or acting. One person that I knew thought that her road to fame would come through a modeling career and meeting Elvis Presley. Instead she found her peace having a family and guiding her children.

Where do we find lasting peace?

Does it come from having the reputation that we are the best hostess on the block?

Does it come from volunteering to do work for many worthy organizations?

Let us look at our road map to peace and see how we can get on the right road:

"I will both lie down in peace, and sleep; For You alone, O Lord, make me dwell in safety."[4]

Do you lie down at night with total peace, or are you nervous about the path that you are following?

Are you caught in a web of deception as in *Charlotte's Web*, the book that my sister reads to her students in elementary school? Is your web similar to the web that restricted Elvis—he had to rent the whole theatre to have peace from the mobs of followers who adored him?

This web of success's tight grip can be smothering.

Or, is your web, a cobweb of failure? Everything you try fails. You have failed so much in the past that you tell yourself that you are not worth anything to anybody. You may as well leave your wife and family and take a road to another state where no one will recognize you. You tell yourself that your children will be better off without you.

Is this the net that surrounds you?

"…In the net which they hid, their own foot is caught."[5]

We all desire that our lives will have purpose—to have some meaning in it. We want names to live on so we name tall building for important people. We built statues to fallen heroes. We build museums to house the memorabilia of our past presidents. We have buildings in Washington for President Jefferson, Lincoln, and the Washington Monument.

We even have 365 steps in the Capital building to represent each day of the year.

Still fame and glory—buildings named after us cannot bring us inner peace.

Perhaps, you have no peace of mind because what binds you in its tight grip has nothing to do with success or failure—perhaps you are bound in a web of fear—fear of the unknown, fear of job change, fear of moving to a new location with better opportunity for employment. The list of fear goes on and on.

You may be afraid that someone will discover something that you did in the past. You have covered the facts for years, and the weight of discovery is almost more than you can tolerate.

You carry a heavy load.

Physical abuse may be your net. You were abused as a young child, and you have never been able to wipe the terrible thoughts from your mind.

You feel as if this strong spider's web of despair and hopelessness has you in its net because somehow you have told yourself that it was your fault. You didn't do something right or he wouldn't have hurt you. You push it to the back of your mind, pretend that it never happened, and go on with your life.

Maybe it was incest, and you feel as if you have a chain around your heart much heavier than a rope, a net, or a web. You think that God has forgotten you—that He could never forgive you.

A personality flaw might be the woolen blanket that is smothering you, or you may feel as if you are locked in a trunk with no hope that anyone will find the right key and unlock your personal prison.

Your hurt is far deeper than sadness.

Your hurt is so deep that you think the only hope for you is the coffin. Death would be a relief. You are deeply depressed and do not want to leave your house, or see anyone. You do not feel like dressing to go to your job.

Everything seems futile.

Life not longer has purpose.

Sin, depression, and despair are chasm that only God can help you to cross, but He has made a path for you to take to find Him and to find total peace.

Jesus can break the:

- Web of Hate
- Web of Self Pity
- Web of Cheating
- Web of Bad Habits
- Web of Gambling
- Web of Cursing
- Web of Drug Abuse
- Web of Bitterness
- Web of Doubt

What may have you bound is a physical illness—a sickness that just gradually eats away at your muscles, your limbs, or your whole body. Limbs once youthful and useful no longer operate correctly for you. Each month you lose muscle functions that you once took for granted.

You are handicapped by this illness.

Maybe CANCER has you bound by the fear of death—the unknown.

Maybe a HEART ATTACK has left you with limitations.

There is good news!

You can unload your fear by turning to God for strength. You can replace your problem by taking the path to God.

Call upon God.

Your circumstances may not change, but your feeling of despair will.

Everything in creation was made to give. Trees give shade. Fruit trees give delicious fruit. Clouds give rain. The sun gives sunshine.

Give the Lord your sinful nature. Ask for his forgiveness.

Then accept it and give Him your

- Praise
- Love
- Heart
- Mind
- Ambitions
- Desires
- Thoughts
- Thanks And Praise

Make peace with yourself.

Make peace with your Creator.

"....Let the weak say, I am strong."[6]

If the web or net that has you bound is the iron bars of prison, and you have committed a serious crime; you are locked behind bars and cannot get out. You must serve your time. When you do leave prison, follow a different path. Do not associate with the crowd that helped you get in prison. Just "Leave prison by a different path."[7]

Turn to God.

Why?

This one verse would be enough reason to look to Jesus: "For the Lord watches over all the plans and paths of godly men, but the paths of the godless lead to doom."[8]

Time with the Master

- What has you in its tight grip? What has you in a web of despair?

- How can you obtain help?

BY SINCERELY PRAYING THE FOLLOWING WORDS WITH ME TODAY:

Jesus, beginning today I desire to have inner peace. Please forgive me of my sins and place your peace within my heart. I will praise you for making me a different person and for giving me a new feeling of joy and peace. Place me on the path that you desire me to follow. Thank you for your presence in my heart and life. I know that you will make a big difference in my daily life. Amen.

12

Pathway to Friendship

Friendship
by JAN WEBER

Some Friends are for a season;
Some Friends are of different kinds.
God gives them all to us—
Always at just the right time!
They are special, they are precious.
They are Gifts from above.
They share our joy, our pain,
And especially our love.
We couldn't do with them;
They add so much spice.
Thank you God for sending
These friends into our life.

A friend of over thirty years shared that she was having a lot of pain and discomfort from acid reflux. Since she had also had some other physical problems, it appeared that these problems should stop and that she should get on with her life.

It was during this time, that she wrote the beautiful poem above and gave it to me.

She was always giving me a book and writing a poem in the inside cover. I treasured her poems, but I treasured her friendship even more.

There are times when we think that it can't get rougher, but the path gets tougher.

During the hot summer of 1945, I laid eyes on Claudette Jolly for the first time. This visitor to Savannah with her round face and snapping, bright eyes had no idea what a "tad" was or where "over yonder" referred to.

Being a true southern girl, I had heard these words from the time I learned to talk. They made perfect sense to me. This was really the first time that I was made aware of our colloquialism.

Everybody in my small southern world knew what I meant when I said, "Scoot over a tad; I don't have enough room."

Of course, it meant a few inches—maybe six, maybe eight— somewhere in that ball game.

A southern lad and lass learned at an early age that "over yonder" meant whatever you wanted it to mean when you said, "Let's go over yonder."

Claudette had no clue.

She was raised with no idea of distance, but boy did I teach her about southern ways that one summer. She ended up being a fast learner the year she lived with her Aunt Odessa in Tennessee.

Every girl should meet one new friend every year and never lose them like I lost Claudette and Edith Davis. I had the joy of going to school with Edith through the fourth grade until her parents moved away. I still remember her warm smile and those strawberry blonde curls hanging down to her shoulders. Her smile could light up a third-grade classroom.

To me she was beautiful and unique. I loved playing with Edith and working math problems with her for our teacher Miss Katie Dixon.

I had no friends at school with a totally round face like Claudette. I had friends with long faces, rectangular faces, long faces with high foreheads, but never a real r-o-u-n-d one until that summer.

I wondered about her after she returned to her home in Montana that fall to begin the next school term. We had so many fun times exploring in Patterson Woods surrounding my house and wading through and the branches—swinging in the front porch swing.

We even had a jacket just alike—red and navy blue. We look liked two sailors as we went to the carnival and smiled into the machine and paid our quarter to see our picture.

That picture that I have kept through the years is the only proof I have that my friend really existed—one photo at a passing carnival.

I wondered if she married, had children and grandchildren. I wondered where she lived today and if she grew up with a firm faith in God.

At the age of ten you never discuss the deeper, fundamental aspects of life, heaven, and the hereafter. We just had a summer of childish fun on the acres of wooded land around the old two-storied house with a huge porch on two sides and a large, white wooden porch swing wide enough to seat three people.

Life was safe, and we could explore without any threat. It was a good time to be a child, and I formed a bond of love with her that still remains even though I have not seen or heard from her in over fifty years.

I guess that is how it is with God. His love is everlasting and unending. He never forgets to be our very best friend. The difference is that He is never far from us and can be in our hearts constantly.

I am reminded of two other bonds of friendship on the pathway through life that started at an early age—one from birth, or at least from my earliest remembrance, the other from grade nine in high school—Rebecca Ross and Martha Nell Horton.

The wonderful aspect of a Christian life is enjoying the friends that are sprinkled along the way.

Just as my friendship with Becky was close, so were our homes and families. There were three houses separating Rebecca and me; one mile separated me from Nell.

Rebecca and I played together before kindergarten and went through school, grades one through twelve, in the same school. Becky with her jet-black hair framing her pretty face and Nell, who was a year behind us in school, with her light, honey-colored hair and sweet, friendly disposition, were treasured friends.

Becky and I went to church four times a week—twice on Sunday, on Wednesday night, and on Saturday night to a youth meeting. Nell soon joined us, and we enjoyed the camaraderie of growing up in a wholesome, Christian environment.

Going to church was never a chore but a much-looked-forward-to event. Memorizing Bible verses and having contests to see who could quote the most verses helped to cause our friendships to bond and expand. In this contest, if you could not think of another verse to quote, you had to take your seat and the last one standing was the winner.

I always thrived on competition, because I had a little of my father's disposition. He was very competitive in the field of sports—especially baseball. The Brooklyn Dodgers offered him a contract as a young man, but since he was married, he had to turn it down.

Again, the 40's and the 50's was a good time for these two friends to "sprout wings" and to enjoy learning now to drive. Nell's father would not let Nell drive his truck, but since Becky was a year older, he allowed her to drive the two of them to the Cherry's Truck Stop for hamburgers and warm pecan pie.

Pathway to Friendship

It was on one of these trips when Becky was spending the night with Nell that Becky backed his truck into another car at Cherry's Restaurant. The two of them were scared to tell him, but he just said that it could happen to anybody.

We never need to be afraid to tell our heavenly father how we feel and what our fears are. He will understand and lead us.

After our senior trip to Daytona Beach, Florida, and after graduation, we went our own ways. I left for college at Vanderbilt, and Becky worked for the local dentist, Dr. Sinquefield. Later, she married her high school sweetheart, Wallace Sibley. Nell married Wallace's friend from Memphis, Lloyd Hawkins.

I recognized that this bond of love between friends is described in I Samuel 18. Today over forty years later, we are still going to the same church, in fact, last night the three of us were seated side by side in the sanctuary. At the end of the service, our pastor asked us to choose one section of the auditorium if we wanted to pray for the youth of the church, another area to go for prayer for the Sunday service, another place for prayer for our pastors, and a fourth area to pray that souls would be saved. We each moved from our seats and went to a different section to pray.

We serve an awesome God who has guided us on our paths through life in the same town of five thousand and today in the same church.

"The path of the godly leads away from evil; he who follows that path is safe."[1]

When Nell, Becky, or I experience serious situations which call for prayer, we call each other day or night. This has been a strong source of strength for all three. We know that each request will be taken to the throne of God with expediency. This is a comfort and an encouragement.

"Anxious hearts are very heavy but a word of encouragement does wonders!"[2]

As friends, we stand ready for each other—on call for prayer, because we have read that "God delights in those who keep their promises, and abhors those who don't."[3]

Preparing our hearts for prayer is like a farmer preparing his field for springtime planting—first you clear the land, make straight rows, and fertilize the soil. You spend more time in preparation than in sewing the seeds.

The same is true of preparing the heart. You read God's word and remove the bad thoughts. "Finally, brethren, whatsoever things are true, whatsoever things are honest, whatsoever things are just, whatsoever things are pure, whatsoever things are lovely, whatsoever things are of a good report; if there by any virtue, and if there be any praise, think on these things."[4]

I was in bed at our winter home in Florida when my cell phone pierced the quiet of that Saturday night. I grabbed for the receiver and answered. My sister had bad news. Becky had just been diagnosed with an aneurysm of the brain and would undergo surgery Sunday morning at 10:00 a.m.

After the information was absorbed by my shocked brain, I knew that I had a task to accomplish—I had to pray until I touched God for Him to keep Becky safe during surgery.

I prayed for a long period and then went back to sleep. My sleep was interrupted again at 4:00 a.m.—not by a ringing telephone but just by my awareness that I needed to pray again.

As I lay in my bed and prayed from four to five o'clock, I knew that I had not let my friend down. I have covered her with a banner of love and prayer.

It had been hard for me to understand why both of my closest friends—Becky and Nell—had both had aneurysms of the brain and had gone through the same surgery a few years apart, but I did not question that God had been with both of them.

They had both been there for me when my appendix ruptured a few years ago. In fact, I had over thirty friends who had gathered at Pickwick Inn that day and were praying for my health even before the proper diagnosis came.

We need that bubble of protection when we are too sick to pray for ourselves. A bubble has all the colors of the rainbow in it, so I like to equate it with the promises of God—a rainbow was a symbol of God's promise to mankind.

I remembered the summer of 1950.

Verlene had been graduated from high school and was working at Burdine's in Miami, Florida, while living with our grandmother. Mother and I were also visiting my grandmother for the summer.

Weeks passed. Verlene's routine of work followed a bus ride to downtown Miami, but payday dulled the pain of the routine workday. She was working to purchase her college wardrobe by operating the elevator.

Verlene had made a new friend at church; her name was Guyla Mae Swinford. Although the friendship was in the inchoate stage, Verlene found a kindred spirit in Guyla Mae, who was so open, honest, friendly, and trusting. Guyla saw only the good in everyone. Her infectious laughter drew Verlene like a magnet. The two of them saw each other every Sunday during Sunday school and formed a friendship.

My sister never met a stranger. Friendliness just came easy for she was a big talker. A stranger would discover that they were revealing problems and personal information without realizing it, because of her honest, dark-brown, sparkling eyes under a darker brown eyebrow.

Her caring disposition and exhilaration gave vivacity to their dull routine while riding the elevator. Her "good morning" and "how are you today?" was said in such a melodious manner that it became the glue that the elderly sales ladies needed to explain to Verlene that the cat had just died, or their friend had been in a car wreck. She was easy to confine in with her ready smile and lovely face crowned with a wealth of freckles.

She had a funny way of arching her eyebrow and using her hands when she talked. She always talked with her hands.

Saturday was Verlene's day to dawdle leisurely washing and ironing her clothes, to go to the beach with Guyla Mae, or to drive Mama's car so that the whole group could see the glass-bottom bridges on the way to Key West.

Although their friendship was forged in one summer, it lasted for a few years until they gradually drifted apart. Verlene stayed in touch until after they were both married and still talks about her.

Although flowers die and leaves change colors and drop from the trees, memories of friendship never fade or totally dissolve. They just mellow with the years.

Although there was a span of five years between my sister and me, our relationship was closer than the years, because Verlene treated me as a peer. This bond of blood and friendship tightened as we both accepted Christ in the same revival and as we shared friends from a wide age range.

Our friends affect our lives—we, in turn, have an equal effect on them. The Bible states, "Iron sharpeneth iron; so a man sharpeneth the countenance of his friends."[5]

Discussions with our friends can inspire and encourage us. My mother used to tell me when I was a teenager that I would be known by the friends with whom I associated.

My mother firmly guided us both—making sure that we selected friends with good reputations. At times we thought that she was too harsh, but later as a parent myself, I found myself doing the same thing—modeling my mother's pattern.

Another of her favorite sayings was "birds of a feather stick together." The Bible words it in the following manner:

"A mirror reflects a man's face, but what he is really like is shown by the kind of friends he chooses."[6]

I trust my friends.

In this age when children are told not to trust strangers, we see the dye being cast to break the bond of new friendships. On my long street, I see for sale signs posted periodically in front yards. People are mobile; they come and go in today's transient society and long friendships become more rare.

Tenaciously, I hold on to my friends with a firm grip. They are priceless.

The poem at the beginning of this chapter and this poem at the end were given to me by the same friend. Her husband is a minister in Colorado. I remember a time when my father died that I called him for prayer.

I also called him during the middle of the night when there was another death in the family. Their friendship was constant, unwavering, and true.

When I think of Biblical friends, my mind goes to Jonathan and David. They had a unique bond of friendship. When I think of people who lived earlier, I think of Edison and Ford. These two men met in 1896 at a convention in New York City.

Henry Ford, who was born near Detroit and who was working on a horseless carriage, impressed the famous Thomas Edison. The two inventors formed a friendship that lasted for the rest of their lives—in fact they both had homes side by side in Ft. Myers, Florida. I especially enjoy seeing these two homes lighted for the Christmas season. All the lights down McGregor Avenue with all its stately palms are a sight to behold.

This second Jan Weber poem reminds me of these two famous men—Edison and Ford—and the rare bond that existed between the two.

Friendship
by JAN WEBER

Friendship for now or for all time
What a wonderful gift this friend in kind.
To share in our hurts, our joys and our tears
Having a true friend to last through the years
Why have a friend? Why share your life?
Why make the effort through good times or strife?
Because the blessing of friendship given
Have their rewards oft' seen only in heaven.
For a friendship true is one that will last

Paths That Cross

Where heartaches are shared and hurts kept in the past.
So when my heart is troubled where can I go
To this friend so special, this person I know.
Through a relationship so sweet 'tis surely from God
'Twill never lessen on this long road we trod.

Time with the Master

- What types of friendship have you formed?

- Think of your friends; do you have Christian friends that you can call on day or night that would pray in a time of emergency?

- If the answer is no— why is it no?

- Can you make a conscious effort to form friendship with people who have a strong faith in God?

READ AND PRAY THIS PRAYER WITH ME:

Jesus, help me to choose my friends wisely. I need your help doing this. I have not always made wise decisions in my choice up to this time. Many of my friends live on the wild side of life and I have followed them by doing many things that I am not proud of. I need your help starting today. Thank you for being my friend as I follow YOUR PATH from this day forward. Amen.

13

Path to Protection

A mile west of my childhood home, the Tennessee River, with all its stark beauty, flowed north and glistened like spun gold as the sun beamed down on the water on warm summer days. Its currents were full of pure magic as boats skimmed over the dark green waters. My hometown was full of the drama of stories about the strong-willed, southern characters with their tenacity and charm who lived within my circle and who touched my life.

The flow of hot lead caught my attention as I slammed the screen door leading from the back porch to the yard where Daddy was holding cones of paper that he was filling with the melted lead to form weights for his rod and rill.

My day was full of watching his ingenuity and soaking in his knowledge. If you didn't have a store-bought item, just make it was his motto.

I was fascinated by two things—his stories from the past and his present task. I knew that when the lead cooled, I would get to go fishing with him.

I was always ready for adventure of any type, and this future trip to the river or a nearby creek was high adventure for me.

On this particular day, he chose Horse Creek over the Tennessee River. I really didn't care where we went. I just liked being around the water and being with my dad.

I jumped in the truck with him and was set for a Saturday adventure at the edge of the creek. After traveling about half a mile, he parked his truck at the side of Highway 64 and we strolled through the grassy path that led to the creek.

On that hot summer day the heat index was high but the trees along the bank of the river formed a shade for the two expectant fishermen—of course, I just sat and watched.

The shadows of trees fell over the green murky water in the center of the stream. It was quite muddy along the bank but the flowing waters got deep very fast so I was not permitted to swim in this stream. Just watching him catch catfish and string them up before throwing them back into the water until we went home was fun for his youngest daughter.

All the catfish that he caught that day would become our dinner that night after he cut off their heads and tails, skinned them, and notched each fish at an angle on both sides. It was mother's task to heat the grease and fry the catfish.

Mother probably used lard because it was cheaper in the 1940's and monies were not plentiful. Mother even had hens and chickens; we ate the chickens and she sold the extra eggs. Eggs were a bargaining commodity in those years. My grandfather lived on a farm and when I was visiting him on Saturday I would meet the peddler on his route from Burnt Church and purchase a BB bat sucker, peanut butter kisses, or Tootsie rolls in exchange for some eggs.

I looked at the string of fish as my dad declared that he was through for the day. I trudged along beside him trying to take large steps like he did to keep up with him. About half of the way through the field that was surrounded with a barbed-wire fence, he grabbed my hand and yelled, "Run, Betty."

Instantly I obeyed. Behind me I heard a loud snorting noise. He reached down with his strong tanned arms and lifted me over the fence as he pushed the wire down and straddled the fence.

I was safe that day from the mad bull in J. I. Bell's field.

Isn't that just like God? When He sees danger on our path, He reaches down and lifts us over the treacherous waters in our life and places us in a safe spot.

God "defends all who come to him for protection."[1]

Yes, later as I became an elementary principal, I tried to see that each student was in a secure and safe educational environment. The classrooms of the 60's, 70's, and 80's were turbulent years of change.

Students demanded to wear tops with their navels showing and some boys would wear fishnet tops with their nipples showing through. Dress codes changed. Students were permitted to wear jeans to school every day of the week.

High school students demanded to eat lunch off campus.

Parents demanded that grades be altered and standards lowered so that a student with fragile ego would not be "ruined for life."

Teachers demanded to wear pants suits. Teacher unions fought this fight for them and won. This was a big deal in the early 70's when I taught at Wooddale High School in Memphis, Tennessee.

Funny how times change!

The things that seemed important at that time are just taken for granted in 2005.

The unknown is like the murky waters of Horse Creek, but we do not have to be afraid if "we live within the shadow of the Almighty, sheltered by the God who is above all gods....for he rescues you from every trap, and protects you from the fatal plague....His faithful promises are your armor. Now you don't need to be afraid of the dark any more, nor fear the dangers of the day."[2]

Time with the Master

- Do you know that you are under God's umbrella of protection?

- If not, what steps can you take today to insure his protection?

PRAY THIS PRAYER WITH ME TODAY:

Heavenly Father, I need your covering over my life. I have not been an obedient child, but I want to change. Please give me guidance regarding how to walk in your path. I thank you for hearing me right at this minute. Protect my family as well. In your loving name—the name of Jesus. Amen.

14

Dark Paths

> "O the depth of the riches both of the
> wisdom and knowledge of God!"[1]

One, two—buckle my shoe. Three, four—shut the door. Five, six—pick up sticks. Seven, eight—lay them straight. Nine, ten—a big fat hen.

I don't remember when I first heard this, but I have repeated these words many times while playing as a child. As the years glided by, a child's game becomes real life and the process of daily living takes on a new, deeper role—not longer child's play. Now hard and fast decisions must be made—at home—at work. How do we know that we shall make the right decision?

We need knowledge and wisdom.

Wisdom has many names.

Advice is one of wisdom's names. Another is wise counsel—another good judgment. Even a woodpecker can have good judgment.

On December 28, 2002, my husband and I watched as a woodpecker drilling on a palm tree in Florida made its constant repetitive sound. The bird, with its triangular-shaped head, arrived each afternoon around five o'clock by circling the palm with a peculiar sounding call. He then landed on the tree and hammered away eating insects, I guess.

My husband called for me to bring his digital camera so that he could capture this ritual of moving from side to side of the tree before moving in the hole at the top of the dying tree.

Even this creature formed by God used good judgment by making his nest in a dead palm tree where there was plenty of room for him to sleep in safety each night.

We discovered when the crew came to cut the tree that there was an area of four feet of space inside the tree for the bird. This fellow definitely had a secure place to nest.

God instilled in animals the ability to hunt and select food and to secure a place to live. How did that woodpecker know how to arrive around the same time each afternoon? I could almost set my watch by his afternoon appearances. I could hear his arrival over the hum of the television as he made his circular approach.

I was sad when the work crew came to cut the dead palm, but a special serendipity warmed our hearts when we drove to Tennessee about a week later and turned into the driveway. I heard a hammering sound and looked up at a tree inside our courtyard.

Yes, there was a woodpecker with a triangular-shaped head peeking away at a tall hickory tree.

We had never seen this bird before or since.

But that day it was a special sighting; oh, how I enjoyed seeing that bird!

Wisdom proclaims that she distributes many gifts to individuals; these gifts make people wealthy, because their treasuries are filled to overflowing. The Lord formed wisdom in the beginning before he created the earth, the oceans, and springs of water gushing like fountains overflowing with water, before the hills and mountains were formed.

Read about these facts in the eighth chapter of Proverbs in both The Living Bible and the King James Version—both shed light on how important it is for us to seek and to search for wisdom all the days of our lives.

Wisdom is entirely different from knowledge but both are important, because they piggyback on the other. These two are like a horse and saddle—both necessary for a comfortable ride through life.

The Bible clearly states that if we search for wisdom, we shall find her. With this pool of integrity comes a better, richer existence. She creates a better coexistence for us with relatives, co-workers, friends, and neighbors.

Wisdom gives us a shield of faith that is referred to in Ephesians chapter six. This important armor or shield is needed each day of our lives.

How does an individual find wisdom?

Let's do some Bible research.

The instruction of wisdom starts with the fear of the Lord,[2] but first prepare your heart[3] because what we do always seems to be right in our eyes[4] but the Lord looks into our heart and measures our purity and our spirit[5] —good or bad—evil or kind—bitter or sweet.

How is wisdom found?

It is hard for us not to be in charge.

We want control of

- Our Lives
- Our Plans
- Our Hopes
- Our Dreams

We think we need total control, but this is not what God desires. He wants us to place our dreams in His hands. He wants us to place our profession and works in His hands to become a man or woman of understanding who walks uprightly and searches for righteousness, knowledge, and discernment.[6]

"But when the wise is instructed, he receives knowledge."[7]

I could go to a college classroom, take my seat, open my textbook, and never hear a word of the lecture if my mind is channeled on another train of thought.

I have to make a conscious effort to listen closely to the professor in order to receive the knowledge in his area of expertise. Otherwise, my mind will drift away to other thoughts.

Of course, there is another avenue for learning. I can read the book. But, research indicates that a person learns better if he uses all the senses— to see, hear, feel, smell and taste.

Little ripples fanned out in the center of the water in the canal behind my house. I was standing at the back bedroom window mesmerized by something making tiny waves or ripples in the dark black water.

I watched the motions, almost hypnotized, as I conjured a menagerie of animals in my mind that could indeed make this movement in the shallow but dark water.

I peered through the glass looking for a head to appear.

Minutes passes.

No head!

More minutes pass until time seemed to evaporate into a longer period.

Still no head!

What swimming creature was submerged for so long without breathing?

Suddenly, a round area appeared.

Still no head!

Dark Paths

I looked up at the tall, sun-caressed pine standing stately in the background with its needles swaying like emeralds in the morning breeze.

Surely, this had to be a turtle. I wondered if I had guessed correctly, because by that time the ripple-maker had gone from my view.

I knew that this small canal fed into a large pond where there was a sign posted—DO NOT FEED THE ALLIGATORS.

But these ripples were too small for this to be a man-eating alligator. The week before, I heard on television that a woman had lost her arm while standing by a lake.

Some times dangers come in smaller packages, but that day with the vibrant rays of the light from the sun, the waters did not appear to be dangerous until our neighbor Maxine told us that she saw an alligator come out of concrete culvert.

Illusions and reality can be strange companions.

We can view God through a glass—a mirror—darkly. But, someday we shall see Him face to face without the filtered rays of the sun.

Viewing the ripples in a canal full of rich dirt, sand, and green grasses is similar to seeing the face of our creator through verses in the Bible.

We have to do our research.

Read carefully.

Contemplate the meanings of verses and how they apply to our lives today.

Get help from commentaries.

And pray earnestly.

Pray for guidance.

Then our search for wisdom can illuminate the scriptures before our very eyes.

"The wise man sees evil and dark paths and chooses to stay

away from them."[8]

"The wise man walks in the path that God's right hand enlarged."[9]

"Do not enter the path of the wicked, and do not walk in the way of evil."[10]

When I was teaching vocation office education in high school in the 70's, I overheard a junior telling her friend that she was pregnant.

"Is your Dad upset with you?" the friend questioned.

"Why, no," was her reply, "he is happy 'cause his welfare check will increase with another baby in the family."

I was shocked at her nonchalant reply that day.

This junior had chosen a path to pregnancy at the time in her life when she should be enjoying her life at school—not by being an unwed mother. In class she did not appear to be as mature as her age would indicate. I wondered about the pathway that she had chosen.

Where will she be at the age of forty?

What kind of life will her child have?

What type of role models will he have in his life?

Will she take him to church?

Good people as well as evil people walk on dark paths in their lives.

It was a sad, dark time in my son's life when Higgins was diagnosed with cancer.

This dog was special.

Higgins was so patient.

"Mom, my dog is always glad to see me. He makes no demands on my love," my son said to me.

"I can just say the word Go and he gets so excited. Higgins, do you want to go?"

What a reaction I saw!

That dog would run to the door and stand expectantly.

I never saw an animal with his patience. If my husband had a ball in his hand, Higgins would stand looking at his hand until he threw it. He did not deviate. He waited like the wooden Trojan horse.

We loved that dog like he was a member of our family.

Barry would puree his food for him and check on him during the dark night hours until his death.

He showed Higgins the same patience that Higgins showed Drexel and me.

Some times I wish that I had that much patience with God's plan for my life.

I know that I am a beloved member of God's family, but I also know that dark times happen to Christian people; somehow it is just easier for them since they depend on him to carry the load.

I remember a dark time in the life of an acquaintance; these are the words which she wrote to share with you.

On Friday morning we received a phone call that a large bill had come due and must be taken care of by the close of business that day. Trying not to panic, I started praying that God would have to make this available, or show us what to do to get this bill taken care of. I was holding back a small amount of our Christmas money, but I quickly realized that some presents would have to go back.

Selfishly, I was thinking that with all the money gone, we would not be able to buy a Christmas tree, but realizing how petty that sounded, I keep my thoughts to myself and went on with the day's work.

After the moment of the trauma was passed, I thanked the Lord for helping us at our moment of need and I thanked Him for His graciousness upon us again.

About 9:30 p.m. that night, we received a phone call from

our neighbors next door. They had a gift certificate for a live Christmas tree; seeing that they already had their tree up and decorated, it was going to go to waste. She asked if we would like to have it.

After my husband thanked them and hung up the phone, he shared the conversation with me. I could not believe what I had heard and tears began filling my eyes. I told him about my thoughts earlier that day about a Christmas tree.

All of this has made me realize even deeper how our precious Lord really cares about the little trivial things in our lives.

When we are obedient and open to Him and come to Him first, He has compassion on us even in the smallest desires of our hearts. I will look back on that Christmas with fondness and sorrow, but I will never forget the gift of love that God and our neighbor bestowed upon my children.

✳ ✳ ✳ ✳

Ping, ping, ping, ping—the sound was repeated over and over. What was that sound coming from my sun room?

As I ventured closer, it took on an unfamiliar noise—more like drip—drip—drip with exactly the same interval of silence in between.

I certainly did not like what I spied at the end of my steps—water over my brick floor.

Well, at least it isn't carpet I thought.

There are two sounds that I don't like to hear inside my house—one a dripping sound and the other the sound of a cricket chirping.

Ugh!

Now, I enjoy night sounds in the woods—it's just when I hear it inside my house. That is one path I do not want crickets to take—inside the house.

But when the weather gets cold, crickets seek the warmth of a house. Insects have a way of getting into our house and we have to call for a company to spray.

Sometimes life is like that—full of crickets. Depression has a way of getting into our minds, and we do not function well when we are depressed. All problems loom larger than life.

Life can become full of unpleasant events that chip away at our emotional well being. We may be able to handle a few bad events, but what if they pile up on us? What outlet do we have?

"Keep traveling steadily along his pathway and in due season he will honor you with every blessing."[11]

Time with the Master

- Have you gone through a dark period in your life?

- What helped you?

- Maybe it was a member of your family and you helped them during a rough time; what means did you use to see them through this tough period?

SAY THIS PRAY WITH ME FOR YOURSELF OR A FRIEND:

Jesus, help us during periods of depression, despair and grief. Help us to rely on your strength and not on our own strength. Also let me know how to help others who need it desperately. Amen.

15

A Winding Path Through the Iris

In April the campus was bathed in color. Iris blossoms in variegated colors and hues dotted the landscape of the college campus. The state flower had been given a home on either side of the meandering sidewalk.

As I went to my classes the iris stood at attention and saluted me with its beauty. I saluted back, because I was smitten by the beautiful colors of yellow, purple, white—every variation that could be obtained was planted on campus.

It was the spring and summer of 1955.

Before air conditioning existed in the classrooms or dormitory!

I finished the quarter and enrolled for eighteen hours and paid my tuition of $153. I had a scholarship to help defray some of the expenses and my father gave me an allowance of $10 a week. This was an adequate amount to cover my meals on campus and occasionally to eat at the Toddle House.

Peabody and Vanderbilt had an agreement—you could enroll at either school and take courses on both campuses. Today both schools have merged into one institute.

I registered for Materials and Methods of Teaching English, Business Machines, and Writing for Publication. The now-famous author of historical books, "Dinner at Belmont," and "Home to the Hermitage" was my visiting instructor.

Dr. Alfred Leland Crabb was a prolific author writing about Nashville and the surrounding areas. As he lectured and taught, I could tell that he enjoyed the past history of Tennessee. I was fascinated by his abilities.

I found that I really enjoyed this creative writing course. On one assignment that he had given us to write, he asked me to pick it up in his office. I thought that this was strange, but I went to his office. He handed me the paper with the question, "Did you receive help writing this?"

In the article I had utilized my textbook from the summer before at the University of Memphis where I have taken Roman and Greek Mythology.

I assured him that nobody helped me, and I guess I must have convinced him because I received an A on the course.

I was so startled that I did not even think to tell him about the course; I could not even answer his question about the Roman god of that I had included in the paper.

I knew who God really was, but I understood why the Greeks and Romans thought up a god for everything. I did not know that day this course was one step on the way for preparing me to write books. We don't see the purpose of our choices many times until later. Then we understand God's purpose.

Years later I thought about the time that I was shopping at Chico's and the sales lady asked me to pray for her daughter as she went off to college. She was leaving home for the first time and she wanted a wall of protection around her child.

"I shall pray for your daughter every night for the next seven nights," I replied.

Since seven is God's perfect number which embodies the fullness of God, I felt that I would be placing a wall of protection for her on this new path that she would be traveling on through college.

Time with the Master

- Do you have fears regarding the path your child is on at the present time?

- Can he call on you for help when the going gets rough?

- When is the last time you have requested prayer for your children?

IF THIS IS WHERE YOU ARE IN THIS STAGE OF LIFE, PLEASE PRAY THIS WITH ME:

Heavenly Father, as your child I have the promise of protection for me and for my family. I am asking for you to place a bubble of protection around my children for the next seven months. Allow bible verses that they memorized as a child to pop into their minds each day and allow the Holy Spirit to guide them as they work or play. I thank you for giving me my children, because I realize that they are a gift from you, and I thank you for your blessings this day; you are worthy to be praised. Glory, honor, and power are yours and we worship you. In the name of Jesus—the name above all names. Amen.

16

Roadblocks

A guardrail placed on the Hernando DeSoto Bridge over the mighty Mississippi River in Memphis, Tennessee, was placed there to be a protective device, but on this day death loomed on the horizon.

Another vehicle struck a disabled van and the family members standing between the guardrail and the van. Three people died even though their emergency lights were blinking.

These young victims did not plan to die that afternoon, but their bodies were no match for the massive machine.

At times we can be on guard; other times, events happen without warning.

Yesterday, I was vividly reminded of how close death hovers around us when I turned on the five o'clock news. A two-year-old child, was strapped into a van owned by a local day care center early in the morning and forgotten. The child was found smothered to death when the children started loading on the bus to go home.

That child's roadblock was a seat belt fastened securely across its body. How can people be so careless? I'm sure that the driver did not plan for a death on his bus, but the horrible accident still occurred.

People are human. Mankind is sometimes careless.

Life has its sounds of pleasure, but what about when the sounds of pain and sorrow come?

Have we made provisions for the period in our lives when joy and fun have flown out the exit and are no longer companions?

The time when a dear one dies!

When life is bleak!

When the sun shines outside but does not penetrate our hearts!

What then?

I am reminded of the squirrels around my back yard. In the fall, I hear sounds of bang, r-o-l-l, r-o-l-l as the squirrels climb the large hickory tree with limbs extending over my master bedroom.

As I walked to the sun room, the squirrels were a beehive of activity; knocking the nuts from the branches, gathering them in their mouths, and digging rapidly into the ground in order to store them for a hungry mouth later on.

This saving knowledge of how to get through the cold, icy winter of our lives should be built into our being. Nature provides the food from which animals benefit.

God provides us with the knowledge of how to store up food in our souls. When the need arises, we can call to mind a Bible verse that we memorized which consoles us and gives us hope for a better, brighter tomorrow.

I watched the path of one particular squirrel jumping and scampering up and down the tree; I was fascinated at how skillfully he jumped from the roof to the tree and even went down the wire to the bird feeder in order to eat the bird seeds. He certainly was agile! I was amazed at how tenaciously he hung onto the wire while he ate.

For thirty years, I have viewed the squirrels in this location and have learned a few lessons from them.

Keep your feet on the ground. Do not venture on the asphalt. It is dangerous! I have seen many young squirrels end up dead on the street in front of my house, because they wanted to cross the road to new territory.[2] Store food. Work hard and you will eat well. Be lazy and you may go hungry.

Have we stored up a place that is secure from the storms of life?

Many of us desire to branch out and to venture on the more dangerous, thrilling edge of life by placing ourselves in the middle of the asphalt—in the middle of the action where the lights are low, where drugs abound as the liquor flows and where the music is suggestive and seductive. Our brains are dulled by Satan's intoxication.

We must live life to its fullest!

Get the most out of every day!

Enjoy ourselves!

Pleasure and fun are our gods; no obstacles block our path of sin.

We do not know that there is both pleasure and joy in belonging to Jesus.

There is both security and peace of mind in abiding in the presence of God!

Read about this security in Psalm 91 and allow His holy presence to cover you today.

Do not allow people to place another roadblock on your path. Sin is like that turtle swimming under water; at first, we don't see the end result—we only see the rippling effect. A young student starts skipping classes to hang out with buddies shooting pool. Then this is too tame, so he goes to the night spots in order to see the girly shows. First he may be shy and order 7-Up to drink, but someone laughs at him so he orders liquor.

He becomes intoxicated with pleasure, sex, and alcohol. Soon after he masters his technique, the three become his master.

Now for a deeper degree of fun, he tries crack.

After he masters this art, it becomes his master.

His girl friend becomes pregnant, but he is not ready for marriage. He marries her out of a sense of duty. Now, he has three to support and his crack habit demands more money.

It DEMANDS to be number one before the baby and wife.

He cannot give up all the fun in life, besides he is only nineteen. The baby's crying at night gets on his nerve and gives him a headache. He's not geared for waking up at night and feeding or changing a baby. He leaves all that to the wife.

His job suffers. He is occasionally late and grumpy too. What is a man to do, he must get his rest?

He had to sleep late on Sunday. Besides, church is for old folks who have nothing better to do. He wants to watch sports on Sunday.

His wife complains.

He leaves.

He divorces her and leaves his responsibility to his child.

Now he will be free, but is he?

A guilt complex has attached to his brain. He was raised in church, but he stopped going long ago. He has shunned the friends who used to be a warm blanket of love to him for so long they have given up on even asking him to go to church.

Like the turtle, his head is under water and he is now drowning in sin and guilt.

Nobody really cares.

Roadblocks

His road to recovery has a roadblock across it.

Is there any hope for the future to be brighter?

Yet, on his bed at night he hears the voice of the Holy Spirit instructing him to change his life style and to follow the "straight and narrow path"[1] that he learned about in Sunday school as a small child.

He rolls and tosses at night. He covers his head with a pillow. He is miserable. He tells himself that tomorrow he will change.

Tomorrow always remains in the future.

What is his hope? Only God can change the heart and lives of sinners. We are powerless to change ourselves, but we can make a start by reaching out to him in faith.

Those Bible promises are sure, true, steadfast, and unchanging. "Jesus Christ is the same yesterday and today and forever."[2] He is in control.

Mankind is not in control.

Tenaciously, I hang on to the promises in the Bible—I even bought a book of Bible promises so that I could encourage myself when roadblocks pop up on my journey through life.

I am reminded of a roadblock on Sanibel Island at Ding Darling, a wildlife reserve. As you drive on the newly paved road, there are steel spikes sticking up, similar to those of rental car lots when you enter. The sign explains that you will ruin your tires if you back up.

A few yards further down the road, there is a box with envelopes and a deposit slot for your money.

There is no guard. You are on the honor system.

The winding road leads to many paths and trails, a lookout tower, and wooden bridges out over the waters. As you drive or walk along, you see many people with cameras taking pictures of the eagles, pelicans, pink flamingoes, and other wild life.

You can stop and climb the tower for a higher view, or you can meander down one of the sandy paths for a close-up view of alligators, but the sign says DO NOT FEED THE ALLIGATORS.

If you drive through hastily, you miss seeing a lot of exotic wild birds.

Some of us go through life in high gear. We have no time for getting close to nature, or for walking the shaded paths. Ding Darling always brings me closer to God.

As I climbed the numerous steps to the observation area at the top of the tower, I was out of breath. It took effort, but the view was well worth the energy on my part.

The view from the top cannot be captured any other way. It is the same with staying on the path with God. It takes effort to know God's will for your life.

It takes effort to follow the instructions in Philippians 4:8-9. It takes a real man to be a Christian role model. You have to brush unclean thoughts from you mind daily like you brush your teeth, but you brush because you do not want cavities.

Daily, we use Crest, Colgate, or some other toothpaste to keep our smile attractive. We like white teeth—yellow ones are repulsive in our society.

Daily, we clear away obstacles that come between God and us. We brush away anger, greed, and malice that lodge between our teeth.

We bring out the Listerine to aid in our endeavor to have pleasant smelling breath. Verses are our toothpaste and mouth wash to rid us of bad plaque.

At the end of Ding Darling, there is another roadblock. A man in a uniform stands there asking to see the slip that shows you paid to enter this honor system.

We showed him ours and asked, "Do many people come in without paying?"

His answer surprised me, "About 80%—but they pay much more when they get my ticket."

Some things in life, we pay on the front end; others later.

ETERNAL LIFE IS FREE.

And while we are still going our separate ways and following our daily routine through life in every stage, our "...spiritual strength comes as a gift from God...."[3]

"With Jesus' help we will continually offer our sacrifice of praise to God by telling others of the glory of his name."[4]

Now we can sense the ageless questions of why we were born and what we are doing on earth—where did we come from—where will we go after we die.

What is the purpose for our life?

How should we act?

Who really cares?

Is there more to life than living on this earth?

Is there a God?

How long will we live?

ONLY GOD HAS ALL THE ANSWERS, but at the age of eleven, I discovered the bridge to the One with the answers. My life has never been the same; praise His Holy Name!

Time with the Master

- Name the roadblocks that have hindered you.

- Are you still experiencing one of these roadblocks?

- What can you do to change this situation?

- Can you change the situation, or do you need help from Jesus Christ?

- Ask Him for help if you need it; nobody else needs to know the problems that you carry in your heart; just release them to a loving God.

PRAY THIS PRAYER WITH ME:

Almighty Father and loving, gentle God. Forgive me for not coming to you for help before. I truly need you. Take the burdens that I have been carrying and give me your power and might so that I can be a productive Christian. Thank you for hearing my prayer. In Jesus' name I ask. Amen.

17

Pathfinder

God's path is mighty on the wings of a storm. In a pure white snowstorm, beauty almost blinds the human eye.

Seven of our most highly skilled astronauts were hurled into the heavens on February 1, 2003, when the Columbia exploded. We are brought face to face with our own mortality.

- Why am I here on earth?
- What plans does God have for my life?
- Am I doing what He desires me to do?
- Am I living to bring Him Honor?
- Is He pleased with my efforts?
- Am I bringing forth fruit for the kingdom of God?

These were my questions as I listened intently to the television commentaries. Do you have some of the same questions? Maybe you have never stopped your routine long enough to question your life. Perhaps you have been one of those individuals seeking pleasure every week end. You may have never found the inner peace that comes with forgiveness.

These seven brave astronauts were pathfinders.

I watched in stunned disbelief as I saw the white stream from the space shuttle streaking across the Texas sky. It separated into three streams of vapor. I sat in silence seeing the replays and listening to the breaking news updating what was being broadcast.

Christians all over the United States prayed for the families of these seven. God honored our prayers and placed a peaceful shield around their family members.

Later I saw that God was receiving glory from their lives of faith and from their love for God. Commander Rick Husband was heralded as a strong man of faith who was thankful that God had opened the doors so that he could be a part of the space program.

He had requested that his minister pray with him for the crew of the Columbia before the lift off.

Our lives leave behind us a testimony for good or for evil. A good name is to be chosen over great riches was a statement I had read many times in my Bible.

Commander Husband had been a pathfinder who left behind a good name.

Men at the Space Center planned the course of the Columbia with great care and precision, but "it is not in man that walketh to direct his steps."[1]

Just as I remember where I was the day that the Challenger exploded, I shall always remember that I was in Florida the day that the Columbia followed the same path and disintegrated before my very eyes.

Think back to the first American launched into space in 1961, Alan Shepard, and John Glenn in 1962, the first to orbit the earth. The Wright brothers would be amazed at their achievement of blasting a path in the sky.

Pathfinder

Automobiles were the first major pathfinders followed by the airplane. Telescopes and telephones were the pathfinders of their time. Flying in an airplane brings my self-centered world into perspective like a telescope. My mind, a pathfinder of a sort, can travel back in time like the speed of light to the year 1953—graduation, 1958—wedding, 1978—promotion to elementary principal—on and on it can zero in on events of the past and like a magnet attracts. It clings to my brain until what I am trying to remember is pulled up.

I am sure that this has happened to you. You try to remember a name from the past and presto—hours later it pops into your mind.

Pasteur was a pathfinder as a scientist, as was Marie Curie.

John Greenleaf Whittier penned these words in 1851 in his poem, Wordsworth:

> But that which shares the life of God
> With Him surviveth all.

Like the poem states we can exist forever in eternity, but preparation is essential.

Repairing the Hubble in outer space was another feat of pathfinders. Special training was required for this delicate task. What a shout went out when the job had been completed.

I had turned on the television on June 1, 2003, to watch *60 Minutes*. I watched as detailed pictures of magnificent colors, shapes, and hues were sent from the Hubble back to earth.

Some new cars like the 350Z have a GPS (global positioning service) located in the car. You can key in an address and it tells you how to travel to that street. This gadget is smart, but if human error is involved and you key in the wrong address, it cannot detect human error.

Some individuals devote their life's work to finding ships that lay on the bottom of the sea. They find adventure in the path under water. Others travel to foreign lands seeking their individual pathways of culture, visiting Spain, Italy, France, and other exciting vacation spots.

You can study a nation by following its cultural pathways from the 1700's to the 20th century. You can view the Grand Canyon, Disney World, and the New England states, ride a steamboat on the Mississippi, or take Amtrak across Canada. You will view the path of men and women who lived before and who took the same trail.

When you receive an e-mail, a computer path is created, because a computer leaves a trail.

Recently I completed two computer courses at a nearby college—Windows XP and Microsoft Word. Computer messages have paths to follow and a menu that you must take to get to given information. I decided that these courses were just what I needed to help me through the winter doldrums.

I thought back to the time when I was one of the first high school teachers in Memphis to teach the keypunch to seniors. We learned how to read the punches, but it was a slow process. The punches made no sense to someone who did not know the coded alphabet.

It is the same with the Bible. A sinner cannot understand the meaning of deep scriptures. God uses the simple to confound the wise.

I read in the News-Press about a lawyer with a prestigious law firm who found the unrelenting stress of finding new clients in order to bring in more money for the firm too much to handle. His boss pressured him to resign. This man who previously had a reputation as an unflinching lawyer was now an indecisive person who was having trouble making minor decisions. To receive help, he went to a career advice specialist, who mapped out for him four possible paths.

The irony of this was that even this made him have doubts about what path to follow, but it was the last three sentences in the article that caught my attention: "You make choices and mistakes. You don't turn into a bad or stupid person because of your mistakes. You just learn from them and continue the journey."[2]

Life is a journey with many paths to follow. Some choices are tough to make, but they reap amazing results.

God does not give up on us just because we make mistakes. Many times we are much too hard on ourselves. We buy our adversary's notion that we are not worth anything and that God will not forgive us. The problem is that we do not forgive ourselves.

We buy Satan's ploy.

We go on our way without asking God for forgiveness, and we carry the heavy bowling ball in the center of our conscience. It slides. We catch it and push it back inside our hearts. We continue carrying the ball when relief is waiting for us.

My husband traced his ancestral path from one generation to another. This was a time-consuming task but well worth the effort.

In future generations, what will the path of your life portray to others?

A prominent businessman?

A great philanthropist?

A man who served others well?

An individual who taught Sunday school for decades?

A housewife who raised her children well?

What path will you leave behind, or will you leave a trail of broken promises?

In Hebers Springs, Arkansas, there is an antique shop with items displayed in an old two-story building. All the walls are lined with items as well as on tables throughout the rooms. On the first floor, only a narrow path large enough for two people to explore side by side carries you from room to room.

The owner stated that her husband had built the shelves for her to display her antiques. As I carefully maneuvered my way down the narrow aisle I viewed many items of interest. Decorated plates, cups, bottles, kitchen utensils, a spinning wheel (not for sale), platters, jewelry, and tea towels flooded my path. I found myself in the middle an antique shopper's paradise—a blending of the past to the present.

Some items reminded me of my mother, and how I had thrown away old kitchens utensils, like a hand-cranked egg beater, similar to the one which now was before me.

I did not know that the old items were worth so much. I wonder if the same is true today when we do not really comprehend how valuable the lessons in the Bible really are. The past and the present blend together nicely. Lessons learned from the time that Moses led the children of Israel through the wilderness are pertinent today.

Moses was a pathfinder, a man who discovered a way. Today, shadows of a time long ago appear as whispers across the pebbled sands and dusty trails. There was no straight path for Moses to follow because of the murmuring and complaining of his followers. Look at all the years that the children of Israel wandered in the wilderness because of sin and unbelief. If God's people had just acknowledged him, He could have made their paths straight. They added years of trouble to their lives. The Bible clearly gives us instruction: "In all your ways acknowledge Him, and He will make your paths straight."[3]

What do the words mean in Mark 1:3 and Mark 4:4? What do the words of John the Baptist mean?

Could it mean clean and straighten out your life? Leave off the fifty words or clean out the refrigerator of your heart—could it mean this?

Clean out the mildew from the top shelf of your head.

Clean out those decayed and molded thoughts and ideas that you allow to remain in your brain as you remove the items at the front of the refrigerator.

Look on that second shelf. What does it contain? A six-pack of beer? Look at the next shelf down. Do you see that sealed container of resentment that you have refused to discard? Check its contents.

Why not discard the food and container at the same time and make room for joy, peace, and healthy fresh thoughts?

Some items have long since had out-of-date contents. As you read the labels and check the calories on an item in the grocery store, check the storage area of your heart.

Are you staying fresh by reading and applying the word of God? Inside its covers are recorded events just like the explosion of Columbia and the Challenger—a time when a complete city was destroyed by God as Lot and his wife fled in haste, but she disobeyed and became a pillar of salt.

The tragedy that followed King David after his lust for a married woman became sin. His sexual desire spiraled out of orbit. Let's review the events:

1. David slept with another man's wife.
2. She conceived.
3. He planned for her husband's death in battle by having him sent to the front lines.
4. He married her and other children were born.
5. One son raped his sister.
6. A son plotted against King David and coveted his throne.
7. Following on the heels of sin came murder and death.
8. His young male heir died.
9. David put on sackcloth and ashes and repented.
10. God forgave him.
11. He was restored to God.
12. He continued as king.
13. He desired to build God a house.
14. God would not allow him to build his house because he was a man of war.
15. God chose his son Solomon to build the house.

This story which took place after 1003 B.C. and 995 B.C. was recorded for our benefit thousands of years later. Do we deceive ourselves into thinking that we can escape the sentence and consequences that follow adultery?

In 2 Samuel 11:2, we read of David's evil desire and lust. We read Bathsheba's words: "I am with child," in verse five.

These words unleashed a chain of events that ended in disastrous results.

This same scenario can be viewed daily on television programs for young eyes to see and for young men to follow.

What are adults thinking?

Sin does not change.

God's penalty for sin is death.

The penalty does not change.

One sunny Saturday in May, on the way to attend my high school reunion in 2003, I saw a church sign that caught my eye—OLD PATH BAPTIST CHURCH. Evidentially, the congregation of that church identified with the old ways of religion—the faith of their fathers was a good path to follow; therefore, they named their church as a constant reminder not to stray too far from the faith of Abraham, Isaac, Jacob, and Moses.

Your heart is a pathfinder to salvation. Of course, you have to listen to it to find that joy, like a bubbling spring splashing up within your being.

God's loving kindness endures forever.

Time with the Master

- Have you thought of someone who was a pathfinder in your modern-day world?

- Can you blaze a path like Lewis and Clark so that others can follow you and know God?

PRAY WITH ME TODAY.

Jesus, light my path today. Help me know your ways by giving me a desire to read your word. Keep my heart and desires in line with yours. Allow me to blaze a path that my family could follow. Thank you for hearing my words and for guiding me. Amen.

18

Paths of Evil or Paths of Promise

When we arrive at the fork in the road, which one will we take?

One fork appears to be a scenic trail with a lot of sightseeing—it seems to promise a lot of fun, but when you have traveled miles on this road, you find your spirit grows weary and you find yourself unable to make wise choices. The road becomes steep, dangerous, and narrow. A missed turn and you could plunge to death down a deep gorge.

The birds still sing, the leaves on the tree still sway in the breeze, and the euphonious sound of waterfalls charm you into thinking that you are on the right path until a warning sign appears: 30 MPH.

You find that you have taken the wrong fork in the road, but you tell yourself that it is easier to go on than to go back.

You have been leaving behind a "trail of misery and death"[1] because of your present life style. You drive yourself with selfish ambitions trying to get to the next town or next career step.

The next sign tells you the name of the nearest town—FOLLY. It sounds like an interesting little country town. You continue onward removing the nagging doubt of going back to the fork in the road.

You are only ten miles from Folly and thirty-three miles from DESTRUCTION, the next town.

In little print on the sign someone has written two warnings—you don't have time to read them since you were driving so fast. In fact, you drove right past the road leading to Folly and headed on to the road to DESTRUCTION.

You were young and wanted to try everything that the next town had to offer.

It wasn't what you expected, since it only had three stores, a post office, and a garage.

Maybe the next two towns would offer more. You asked the attendant as he filled your car with gas, "What is the name of the next town?"

"SIN is fifteen miles down the road, and DEATH is twenty-five miles south of here on that road," he pointed to the west.

You do a double take. You wanted no part of the people in Death. Now you are ready to turn around and go back to the fork in the road in order to find the correct way to the town where you had planned to go in the beginning, PROMISE. Your mother had relatives there and you would be given a warm welcome.

Life is sometimes like this. We come to a fork in the road and we make a quick decision to later discover that we are on the wrong road, but we do not want to stop to ask for directions—we continue driving hoping that we are going in the right direction.

When we find that we are on the wrong road, we have lost a lot of time and have to back track.

* * * *

Paths of Evil or Promise

Sin reminds me of chipmunks and azaleas.

My neighbor Elizabeth gave me an azalea plant with colorful pink blossoms. I told my husband to plant it in the place where an old oak tree had once stood. The decayed area seemed to be a fertile place for the plant to grow and could be seen from the back window.

Some chipmunks, which lived in the hillside behind the house, had another idea. They had the run of our back yard. Without my knowledge, day after day they ate away at the roots of the azalea plant until the plant died.

At times, sin is like a chipmunk, which daily eats away at a healthy heart and places seeds of doubt, distrust, and sorrow in our soul until a flourishing, green plant begins to turn brown and dies.

Our minds once full of kindness and goodness contain vices and cruel ideas. Sin's greedy appetite consumes too much of our waking hours.

We need to return to our roots and become a child again.

I am reminded of a story that I heard in Florida about a lonely lady in her late eighties who lived by herself.

One day the doorbell rang; as she opened the door she saw a little boy and girl age four and five standing eagerly on her porch.

She recognized the children who lived in the third house down her street.

"Well, hello," she said. "How can I help you?"

"My husband and I have come to visit you," responded the five-year-old girl.

"Would you like to come in for a glass of lemonade and a chocolate chip cookie?"

Both nodded their heads affirmatively as the girl said, "Why, yes, we would be delighted," and she tugged and pulled her young brother by the arm.

"Would you and your husband like to have a seat on the

couch?" the lady went along with the game.

She made the lemonade and brought it in along with a tray of cookies. The children eagerly ate and drank. The young boy tugged on his sister's arm and whispered into her ear.

"Would you like another glass of lemonade?"

"No, thank you; we have to go home now. My husband just wet his pants."

Sometimes adults make a game of being a "Christian" until something happens in their life that they are not prepared for; then they return to their faith as these two children returned to their home.

Our "playing church" did not keep us from the evil plans and deadly actions that we devised in order to have fun. We walked in darkness without knowing that we were really seeking light until the reality of Isaiah's words soaks our pants like a five-year-old boy and we return home to Jesus for fresh, clean garments of white.

"It is because of all this evil that you aren't finding God's blessings; that's why he doesn't punish those who injure you. No wonder you are in darkness when you expected light. No wonder you are walking in the gloom."[2]

You are like a painter who does not have a drop cloth and you are getting paint all over the floor. Even a droplet of sin stains the carpet and no amount of stain remover will make the carpet of your soul white again.

The drop cloth has holes in it but we did not take time to purchase a new one—we just continue to use the old, ragged one without good results.

Life is like drinking a Pepsi.

My favorite drink is iced tea, but life is more like a Pepsi.

My husband stated, "Betty, you can't tell the difference between Coke and Pepsi."

"I certainly can!"

"If I blindfolded you and gave you a taste of both, I know that you could not tell me which was which."

"Just try it!"

Boy did I step up to the plate and bat a home run! I told him exactly which drink was Pepsi.

Let me tell you the secret. Pepsi is sweeter than coke. Coke just has a different flavor to my taste buds.

When I have Bible reading and prayer time at the beginning of the day, my day runs more smoothly and is sweeter. I am at peace with how the events of the day unfold. I have started my day correctly—I have communicated with the Lord and the day's work is easier.[3]

His faithful promises are covering me. "Now you don't need to be afraid of the dark any more, nor fear the dangers of the day...nor disasters in the morning."[4]

Around 1876, Kate McCormick, a twenty-one-year-old girl from Humboldt, Tennessee, was seduced by a friend of her father. Kate became pregnant. After coming to Memphis and having an abortion, she died. Her mother was notified and identified the body; she placed one single white flower on her daughter and stated that she wanted nothing to do with the body. She walked out without shedding a tear.

The daughter was buried in a crude coffin made of wood.[5]

The path the young girl chose led to danger, because at that time, an abortion was a criminal procedure which often was performed in unsanitary conditions.

In contrast to the evil paths are paths of promise. Billie Cash provides a list of thirty-one promises for our path for this decade—one for each day of the month. In each promise the word righteous is printed in bold letters. A few of those promises contain words or phrases like the following: a tree of life, a green leaf, brings forth wisdom, never be uprooted, a fountain of life, will be a blessing, flourishes, stands firm, shines brightly, great treasure, can sing, and are just.[6]

Billie gives you something that you can trust—promises for the path of the righteous.

What a blessed inheritance the child of God has!

What a covering of love!

What a shelter from the storms of life!

What a blessed assurance!

God's amazing grace!

Just because man breaks his promises to God does not mean that a loving God will break his promises to mankind.[7]

In Romans 2:7-9 we find that evil ways bring sorrow and suffering while the good path of obeying him brings peace, glory, honor, eternal life, and immortality.

One sad example of this is seen in the tombstone that Dorothy Whitaker erected with an inscription reading: BORN: WHO KNOWS/ DIED: WHO CARES[8]

Although Dr. Doty did not make it to our house before my sister was born, when he arrived he pronounced that she was a healthy baby.

My Dad questioned, "How much do I owe you, Dr. Doty?"

"That will be $50, Clyde."

"Don't you think that's a little high for just looking at her?"

"That's what I charge to deliver a baby."

A few years later, my Dad passed Dr. Doty on Highway 64 and saw that he had gone off the road into a ditch.

Dad slowed down his truck and stopped, "Do you want me to pull you out of the ditch?"

"I sure would appreciate it, Clyde."

After getting a rope and placing it around his bumper, he pulled Dr. Doty out of the ditch.

"How much do I owe you?"

Paths of Evil or Promise

Without hesitation, my Dad said, "Fifty dollars."

Dr. Doty chuckled and paid him.

In 1930 that was a lot of money for a hardworking farmer; today we think that the cost of serving the Lord comes at too high a cost. We will have to give up alcohol, sex outside marriage, cursing, gambling, and a myriad of other vices.

But think what we gain!

Time with the Master

- What is standing between you and a total commitment to Jesus?

- Which road are you on at present—road to evil or road to God's promises?

- Is it worth the cost—your eternal soul—to remain on this downward path?

PRAY WITH ME.

Heavenly Father, I desire to follow the path that you have placed before me. Show me the way and change my heart. Amen.

19

PATHS BEFORE THEM

The enemy was quickley approaching behind them when their path led to a dead end—the Red Sea. Certain death seemed inevitable—their journey over when God's miracle occurred, the Red Sea parted and the Children of Israel walked across on dry land.

You have heard the story many times in Sunday school.

Abraham led his only son Isaac to the top of the mount to offer him as a sacrifice. This path was an agonizing one for this father; possibly he made this journey very slowly treasuring the last hour with his child, but God provided a miracle. He provided a substitute when he saw Abraham's faith.

"Do not move the ancient boundary marks."[1]

This verse is causing havoc in Israel and Palestine—greater bitterness today than ever in my lifetime. Who would have thought when I was a high school student that I could turn on the television any day of the week and hear news on CNN regarding ancient landmarks and boundaries!

Events of each day are carried by news commentators giving details of the latest happenings in the Mid-East—five killed when a bomb exploded, eight killed in Gaza, sixteen in Israel, and many others are caught in the cross fire.

Sharon and Abbas spoke on television with each saying that they wanted to live side by side in peace. Peace was their goal. "We have no interest in continuing to struggle with you," Abbas stated on July 2, 2003, with people everywhere watching the broadcast.

News commentators stated that the world had an opportunity for a cease fire—a chance for a clean beginning.

The path to peace today is not as clearly defined as it was in years past. The world grows more and more complicated. This fighting which started with Abraham, Sarah, and Hagar, when she and her child were sent out on an unknown path, spills over even today.

Today with the road map to peace, the United States is trying to bring Israel and Palestine together in order for them to live and work side by side.

As I read Tim LaHaye and Thomas Ice's book *Charting the End Times*, I noticed that the authors described five crowns—Incorruptible Crown, Crown of Life, Crown of Glory, Crown of Righteousness, and Crown of Rejoicing. This whetted my curiosity to continue. I ran the references in my Bible. All of these crowns were depicted in picture form under the heading: The Judgment Seat of Christ.[2]

Many scholars question whether Jesus ever lived. A newly published book grabbed my attention, because it was coauthored by the same writer who gave us major books on the Dead Sea Scrolls, which I viewed on a trip to Jerusalem. This new book is an account of the archaeological discovery of a fragile limestone burial box bearing the inscription "James, son of Joseph, brother of Jesus:" both of which are regarded as authentic by the major scholars in this field—scientific and tangible evidence of the existence of Jesus.[3]

Paths Before Them

On Saturday, June 14, 2003, I read an article in the News-Press with the headline, Sister turning deadly tragedy into triumph of goodness.

Two sisters were following different paths—one to prison and one to receiving first place in competition of the international Future Problem Solving Program, which was held at the University of Connecticut.

Jessica Hill, age 19, was sentenced to life in prison for killing Paul Townsend, age 78, with a gun in 2001.

Monica Hill, age 17, and a senior at North Fort Myers High School produced a video aimed at showing how the availability of guns and teenage rage can wreck lives.

Both girls moved from foster home to foster home, because their father was not a part of their life and their mother had a drug problem and was in jail on many occasions. This home life did not keep Monica from achieving good grades in honors courses and from being captain of the basketball team.

Their paths began together but took different turns in the road—one path to fame, one path to shame. It probably will be a hard process for the older girl to forgive herself for the murder she had committed.

Evil people leave the "path of uprightness, to walk in the ways of darkness."[4]

As I read Max Lucado's article, "Learning to Love," my attention was caught by his answer about how to forgive other people. He stated that we needed to use the 747 principle for forgiveness in Luke 7:47 NIV where it states," He who has been forgiven little loves little." The fact isn't that God won't forgive us, but that we will not accept His forgiveness.[5]

All of the powerful and great actions of God can be traced to His abiding love.

A young man or woman has many choices to make in life. One of these choices is whether to drink alcoholic beverages. The end results of this path can be hallucinations and tremens. Hard liquor causes people to say foolish things that would embarrass them when they were sober.

Read Proverbs 23:33 LB to see the picture of a person with red eyes staggering like a sailor at sea.

Jessie Peters was responsible for the death of General Earl Van Dorn, a Confederate general, who died by a gunshot from a jealous husband after the husband found him at 2:30 p.m. in his wife's bedroom.

Mrs. Peters was quoted as saying, "Now ain't that the devil! A sweetheart killed and a husband run away, all in the same day."[6]

Sin has consequences. The Bible clearly tells us that the wages of sin is Death.

Her path of unfaithfulness led to murder.

Some paths are healing.

Take the path of the five Peabody ducks. In the center of the Peabody lobby, the South's grand hotel that has been home to the famous Peabody ducks since the 1930's, stands a large gold and black marble pool. In the center are golden angels holding a vase that is always full of beautiful live flowers in variegated colors. The sounds of the water fountain forms a pleasant setting for the ducks to waddle from the elevator at 11:00 a.m. each morning.

About seventy-five to a hundred people lined the upper mezzanine and lower lobby with cameras flashing to capture the pleasant scene. The ducks continued to swim in the pool as the crowd dispersed.

I have visited the Peabody on many occasions to show the parade of the ducks to visiting friends. It is always a joy to watch.

Many other paths are healing paths.

At the beauty shop I picked up the February, 2003, issue of *Better Homes and Gardens*, and an article captured my attention. I read what Doug Hall had written about an office in Peconic, New York. The title, "Soothing Views" grabbed me.

As one quietly strolls down a garden path, it can make us sense that our blood pressure is dropping.

He goes on to describe how this garden was divided into "quadrants by brick paths and enclosed with a white picket fence."[7]

A fountain added soothing, splashing sounds.

This garden was placed outside the office of a Long Island psychiatrist, Joanne Woodle, so that the therapeutic efforts could be felt by her patients. She knew the importance of the senses—what the eyes view enters into the heart of man. This is why authorities say that a person who views pornography never gets over the experience.

The article detailed how Joanne chose carefully in order to create a calming palette of colors, especially the blue colors in order to form a therapeutic, serene path.

What about the path before you?

Which path are you on today?

- a path toward peace
- a path of anger
- a path of joy
- a path of love
- a path of bitterness
- a path of loneliness
- a path of isolation
- a path of happiness
- a path of stubbornness
- a path of selfishness

God gives you a choice. Mankind has free will.

Maybe, you are like my husband's antique clock in the den. It sits in the same place on the mantel over the fireplace that it has occupied for about twenty-five years. The ticking of this clock has always been a friendly sound. I enjoyed hearing the chime on the half hours and the gongs for each hour of the day.

But today, it is useless. We had it checked and repaired. My husband carefully oiled it, but it still does not tick.

Are you like our antique clock? What do you need to start you clicking for God? What a benefit and joy you could give others.

My husband was helping with a cemetery census in Hardin County, our place of birth. He asked me to assist him that week. As he called out the names, I recorded each word on each tombstone.

It was a hot task so we took a break and went to a restaurant in Clifton, Tennessee. It was built next to the Tennessee River. Our view was perfect, and we watched a few pleasure boats going up and down the water. We saw the tombstone for T. S. Stribling, the Pulitzer- prize winner, and toured his museum facing the river.

Afterwards, we went back to the cemetery and continued our efforts of recording the exact wording and dates on the tombstones.

The next day, I started itching. A place on my hip turned red. The itching was continuing so I examined the red place and spotted a tick. I was miserable. We tried a couple of ways to remove the tick and finally succeeded.

My next trip was to the doctor to take a shot, because the red circle had enlarged and continued to bother me.

The path down the rows in the graveyard had led to discomfort. My census taking was over. No more ticks for me! I had enough!

I thought back on some of the dates that I had viewed. The time frame indicated that some had died as babies.

My mother's first son did not live and my mother-in-law's first born, twin girls both died after birth. I used to wonder why my aunt Blanche died so young until I read a verse in Isaiah: "The righteous is taken away from the evil to come."[8]

God in His wisdom makes the final decision of when to take us out of the terrible, evil days that are coming when men will cry for death and find no relief from this agony and misery.

Maybe your journey with God has been like this. You came across a few rough paths and you just gave up on God, because your life was not easy. You think that it is too hard to be a Christian.

Remember the words of David: "O Lord, the earth is full of your loving kindness! Teach me your good paths."[9]

The end of the journey is well worth the effort when we shall rest in total peace with Him.

You may have heard the old saying, "I'm so glad to get home that I am glad I went."

I think heaven will exemplify this old saying a thousand times over. Like the old song goes "heaven will surely be worth it all."

That song made me think of my husband's camel-colored pants. I may have washed those pants fifty times, but the crease remains in both legs. It is a permanent crease that cannot be washed out it seems. These pants were worth the price that we paid for them—they wear well.

Remain constant in your faith. It will pay dividends at the end of your life. Resist Satan's alluring, artificial joy. It is not worth the price, but knowing Jesus and finding his path is well worth the time and effort.

"Your words are a flashlight to light the path ahead of me, and keep me from stumbling."[10]

In God's path
His joy is contagious.
His love is everlasting.
His shelter is secure.
His peace is complete.
His presence is comforting.

Time with the Master

- What are you needs at this time?

- How could you become a more productive Christian?

PRAY THIS PRAYER WITH ME.

Jesus, there are times when I am weak, but you are strong. There are times when I am afraid—be with me. There are times when I am not a productive Christian, but I desire to be. Help me to put my desires into action. I thank you for the help that I know is coming just because you said to ask and I could receive. I do believe. Amen

20

Wisdom's Path

If we could learn a lesson from the past, we should review the events of what happened before the dawn of the sun on September 6, 1863, close to Little Rock, Arkansas.

Two Confederate generals who followed similar career paths had a duel and one died.

Brigadier General John Sappington Marmaduke and Brigadier General Lucius Marshall Walker were evenly matched as a dueling pair. Both had attended the U. S. Military Academy at West Point and both came from distinguished families. Both also "followed similar career paths."[1]

Tension between the two surfaced; then Marmaduke implied that Walker had acted cowardly during an attack on Helena, Arkansas.

Correspondence between the two general is recorded along with the events of that morning when Walker was mortally wounded by a shot from a pistol that hit him in the side paralyzing his legs and lodging in the spine.

Walker's body would later be moved from a cemetery in Little Rock to Elmwood Cemetery in Memphis, Tennessee. Marmaduke became governor of Missouri and later wrote to a friend that he wished he had been there. His exact words were "How I prayed for you to be here. If you had been present, the meeting would never have taken place."[2]

Two similar paths had met a fork in the road—one leading to the cemetery and the other to the office of governor.

"Wisdom gives:

- A long, good life
- Riches
- Honor
- Pleasure
- Peace

Wisdom is a tree of life to those who eat her fruit; happy is the man who keeps on eating it. The Lord's wisdom founded the earth; his understanding established all the universe and space. The deep fountains of the earth were broken open by his knowledge, and the skies poured down rain. Have two goals: wisdom—that is, knowing and doing right—and common sense. Don't let them slip away, for they fill you with living energy, and are a feather in your cap. They keep you safe from defeat and disaster and from stumbling off the trail."[3]

Elizabeth George writes about two seasons of her life—the winter of sorrows and the spring of new beginnings. Individuals can walk down two paths on the same day. She asks these questions; "Are you experiencing ending that for the first time seem to have no new beginnings? Are you being pressed to adjust to a new path that leads in directions you did not anticipate or choose? Are you approaching the next bend in the path with some measure of fear?"[4]

We are gently lead by the writer to the Shepherd and to his

promises—His unending love, His everlasting presence, and His faithful guidance.[5]

I am reminded of how Billie Cash in her motherly wisdom guided her son when he was a young child in the ways of the Lord. As a tool to teach her son, she purchased calendars each year with tear-off Bible verses, the date, and a blank writing space.

On January 30 one year the verse was "Show me the path where I should go, O Lord; point out the right road for me to walk. Lead me; teach me; for you are the God who gives me salvation." She lovingly wrote a note to him and passed it on even through his years at the Citadel.[6]

At that time in his life, Billie and Roy never dreamed that he would be used by God in a dangerous territory. Carey was in Iraq as a US Navy Chaplain and prayed with servicemen going on missions as well as baptized some of these young people in Saddam Hussein's palace in Baghdad.

On Easter, this chaplain had a service in Hussein's palace and preached the good news of the Cross and brought Light into Darkness.

"And he shall bring forth thy righteousness as the light...."[7]

It is wonderful that his mother and father built a bridge for him to cross those rivers that come into each life and that he crossed over the bridge to Jesus at an early age.

On June 29, 2003, Carey Cash shared at a church service by relating his experiences about how faithful God was during those dangerous missions when soldiers shared with him how they heard bullets whizzing by their heads and thought they would be hit, but miraculously they came back safely.

This mother's wisdom and use of the verse calendar produced souls in the kingdom of God. How very wise she was! What a wise path she created for her son!

"O my son, be wise and stay in God's Path."[8]

"A wise man is mightier that a strong man. Wisdom is mightier than strength."[9]

"My son, honey whets the appetite, and so does wisdom. When you enjoy becoming wise, there is hope for you! A bright future lies ahead!"[10]

"The Lord, your Redeemer, the Holy one of Israel, says, I am the Lord your God, who punishes you for your own good and leads you along the paths that you should follow."[11]

Wisdom is everlasting. "Does not wisdom cry out. And understanding lift up her voice? She takes her stand on the top of the high hill, beside the way, where the paths meet.[12]

Time with the Master

- What method are you using to teach your children?

- Are you in the season of sorrow or the season of new beginning as a Christian?

  Maybe you classify it more like walking through the fog. The Nubble Light, a lighthouse in York, Maine, has guided many ships safely to shore during periods of fog and storm; God's light is much brighter and will safely guide you in the right path.

- Are you building a bridge to Christ that others may have a safe passage from earth to eternity?

PLEASE PRAY WITH ME:

Jesus, teach me the methods that I should use when instructing my children. I do desire a safe passage for them. I want to build a bridge for them over troubled waters in the future. I desire your guidance, your wisdom, and your love and peace in our family. Amen.

21

Guarding the Path of Minerals

On Tuesday, I usually eat lunch with my friends; one of them is Melba Cole, a fun-loving individual whom I met in 1972. Her husband, Jim, was a chiropractor, but his hobby overshadowed this in my eyes. Jim had searched in many areas of the world for rocks, minerals, and rare stones.

Dr. Jim had a wide net of influence in the state of Tennessee in his profession and had encouraged sixty young men to become chiropractors. Of 1,100 licensed chiropractors, his was Number 67 in the state.

Dr. Jim was spending the week at his cabin in Arkansas playing with grandchildren and talking about where he had located minerals and rocks in the past. Although he had been to Spain, the minerals that he had dug out of the ground in Arkansas and Tennessee were dear to him; he had boxed, labeled, and stored them—some in beautiful, colorful showcases. This had been a life-time passion of this former fighter pilot who had served in World War II and Korea.

Jim had been going through the darkest path of his life battling the dreaded cancer.

That day he dropped his head on the table in front of him and said to his loved ones who asked him, "What is wrong?"

"I can't hear the birds sing—it's time to go home."

A few days later, he ventured on a new path—he was viewing precious stones indeed: jasper, sapphires, emeralds, topaz, amethyst, and pearl, as recorded in Rev. 21:18-21.

His eyes for the first time were viewing gold so pure that it looked like clear, transparent glass. The blue-gray quartz was the most beautiful that can be imagined. It's like the child's song; I know because the Bible tells me so.

Dr. Jim "walked with God," and after his last trip on the mission field to help the poor and needy—people who had no monies to pay for medical services, he came home with a new zeal and new passion to share his testimony of God's great love.

His last journey did not scare him—he was ready for a path that did not have rugged rocks, deep gorges, ravines filled with murky, black water, or dirty diggings of minerals and rocks.

Sometimes our pathway leads us in the valley of the shadow of death.

His wife shared with me that the only color she saw when she opened her closet was black. There was no color in her life after Jim was gone. The color had been ripped out of her heart so every time she dressed, she chose black. She was glued to a black path!

The beauty of color had flowed like a stream during her happy days, but now sadness had created a gulf of black. She had little desire to socialize. She missed him the most when she was at the table drinking coffee—the hours which once had passed so swiftly, now dragged across the daytime hours.

Guarding the Path

A long-time friend, from Punta Gorda, Florida, invited her to visit the sunshine state known for oranges and grapefruits. When Melba visited Sanibel Island, she felt that the color had returned to her life and that she was going to make it—make all those decisions by herself regarding filing income taxes, rental property, which items to sell, and which to keep. Jim's rock collection had been extensive.

She laughingly told me that she now saw color when she opened her closet door, and what a joy it was to feel God's awesome love for her. She had always felt his nearness but never so much as she did during this period of sorrow.

When I asked her if I could share her experience, she replied, "Yes, because I feel His presence so close to my heart that I will never be totally alone."

That's how close God is— inside our hearts, not above our heads He is our light and lamp.[1]

Where do individuals get their drive to achieve goals in life? Louisa May Alcott wrote *Little Women* in 1868 in order to help her family financially.

Ernest Hemingway, William Faulkner, Robert Frost, and Eugene O'Neill had a myriad of reasons to write. Also we remember Henry Longfellow, Walt Whitman, Emily Dickinson, Edgar Allan Poe, and Mark Twain—each of which lead us on a journey of joy as we read their poetry and literature.

What drive spurred Alexander the Great to conquer much of the then civilized world and to become one of the greatest generals in our history books?

What drive pushed Elvis Presley? Personal friends who worked and sang with him stated that after his concerts he wanted them to sing gospel songs for hours. They sang until the early hours of the morning. This, they believed, was his first love—the path he really wanted to follow.

What goals have we accomplished and what goals are in the future for us to achieve?

Today, what book do we purchase the most? I have heard that it is the Bible, the most sold book of our time.

Who are the real heroes? Moses? Abraham? King David? Solomon? Paul? Matthew? John? Luke? Mark?

Not many of us will ever be called by our first name alone. There are hundreds of Betty's—so who would know which one we are referring to if we wrote about ourselves using only the first name? But we can achieve goals by walking on the path that God places before us each day. We can be great in His Kingdom. He calls us by our first name; in fact, He knew us while we were still in our mother's womb.

It is never too late!

Satan is a master at manipulating our time and our thoughts; he is good at scheduling—scheduling sex on television, killing and fighting, physical and sexual abuse—we are even bombarded with suggestive sex on computers. It flashes on the monitor—place your mouse on this and left click this icon and enjoy elicit pictures of sin.

Today, some of us spend more time on our computers than we spend reading the Bible. The most important aspect of our lives has been relegated to the back of our priorities until all other roads have been explored.

We tell ourselves that after I am promoted, I will attend church. After my children are grown and I no longer have to work two jobs, I will find a church we tell ourselves. I just don't have time now, but in the future, I know I'll have more time. But the backpack that we carry grows heavier every day from the bricks of guilt that we carry.

Man does what he wants—he places others things at the top of his to-do list while the guide book to heaven remains on the table by the bed or on the shelf where he placed it when it was passed down to him from his parents.

Another brick of guilt has been added to the bricks of jealousy, pride, revenge, greed, unbelief, cheating, bitterness, and stubbornness.

The backpack gets heavier and heavier.

Guarding the Path

At times, I try to make airplane trips hard by carrying too much luggage on my trips overseas, because I think that I must take nuts, and peanut butter and crackers. I don't want to go hungry. The thing in this life that I am most hungry for is to know more and more about God.

I am a creature of habit—I have lived in the same house for thirty years, worked on the same job for thirty years, and attended the same church for an equal number. Following this curving road which I have followed for fifty years is not habit. A stronger zeal is in my heart today than when I accepted Christ as my Savior at the age of eleven.

The excitement is heightened! The desire to read His word is far greater than when I first read the Bible from Genesis to Revelation in college. This path of symbols was placed in the Bible for us for this time in history—it is pertinent to current events. We must study Revelation!

Facts it contains grow clearer. This path has taken on additional excitement as I study the meaning of the number seven in Revelation—the seven candlesticks, the seven stars. He clearly explains in the scriptures that the two are symbolic of the churches and angels, but it goes deeper, as John writes about the seven main characters on the scene, the seven seals, seven trumpets, and seven bowls. As we study these judgments, they take on more meaning as the conflict in the Middle East looms larger and the news commentators proclaim news alerts on CNN and Headline News.

We may not totally comprehend the politics of the time, but we can clearly discern that there is more and more talk of WAR while the world desires PEACE.

Why do we have to worry about chemical death in a bottle? Nerve agents? Nuclear weapons? Biological weapons? Why do 30 million people in Africa have AIDS? Why do we have 50,000 federal screeners in airports? Why are women strapping bombs on their body and blowing themselves up in Moscow and Israel?

The Bible states that we shall always have this element of evil in our society, but we can give our backpack to Jesus to carry for us.

He can become:

- Our Everlasting Father
- Our Almighty God
- Our Prince of Peace
- Our Shepherd
- Our Lily of the Valley
- Our Bright Morning Star
- Our Faithful
- Our Holy One
- Our Alpha
- Our Omega
- Our Abba Father
- Our Jehovah

The final conflict belongs to God.

As His children, we are safe.

The most beautiful rainbow that I have ever seen was viewed as my husband drove on highway I85 in Montgomery, Alabama. First it appeared faintly; then it took on vibrant, brilliant colors until it faded from the sky only minutes later. We saw the glory of God and were reminded of His promise that day in February that the world would never be destroyed again by a flood. The next time it will be by fire.

Our lives are brief in the span of time, but eternity faces each of us. As you know, eternity is forever and that is a long time to be with our loved ones in harmony with God.

"Since we have such a huge crowd of men of faith watching us from the grandstands, let us strip off anything that slows us down or holds us back. Especially those sins that wrap themselves so tightly around our feet and trip us. Let us run with patience the particular race that God has set before us."[2]

Time with the Master

- What do you fear most?

- What is holding you back from a secure walk with God?

    a. Prayer?
    b. A time for Bible reading?

- What is the burden that you are carrying on your back?

PRAY WITH ME:

Heavenly Father, I desire to trust and to follow you. Deliver me from the fear of the unknown and give me an assurance that you are with me this day. Help me to understand the Bible as I read your word. Also, help me to give you the burdens that I am carrying this day. I need a lighter load. I will praise you and give you glory because you alone are holy. Thank you for an answer to my prayer. Amen.

22

Parallel Paths that Never Cross

> Thou hast fenced up my ways, made my paths crooked,
> To keep my wand'ring eyes fixed on Thee,
> To make me what I was not, humble, patient;
> To draw my heart from earthly love to Thee.[1]

Life is a cornucopia containing a potpourri of miscellaneous activities, events, and experiences. An individual may hide unhappiness behind a valiant veneer with a stoic face. A pantomime of moments of sadness and joy all rolled into one can at times overload our minds. Sometimes we need a respite from nocturnal solitude—from images from the past.

As the poem above stated, sometimes our paths may be crooked to teach us humility and patience. It is up to us to reverse this impatience into a positive, powerful force of energy that will propel us to a closer relationship with Jesus.

When we accept Christ, we do not need to fold away our dreams—merely turn them over to a better pilot—a master who does not pinion us by force but with an altruistic love and caring hand.

Our future does not need to be an existential, cloudy mystery; we can uncover astral displays of truth and eternal revelations by simply reading books.

I have found *Matthew Henry's Commentaries* to be an excellent source for me when I do not understand a Bible verse. We need to form a lifelong habit of reading.

Or, are you determined to ride through life turning and twisting down every dead end path along your way? Are you like a raven flying in the night or like a lamb running on the steep hillside determined to chart your own course? You don't desire a straight path—that would be boring! Whatever is over the next hill is the most important adventure for the moment.

The day-by-day routine in not a security to you—it is a full-blown depression.

Phew! Another routine, uneventful day holds no excitement, and the nights hold crazy dreams with galactic figures, ugly shades of dark green and confusing characters. I have often wondered how people endure wakeful nights without prayer.

> If peace be in the heart,
> The wildest winter storm is full of solemn beauty,
> The midnight flash but shows the path of duty,
> Each living creature tells some new and joyous story,
> The very trees and stones all catch a ray of glory,
> If peace be in the heart.[2]

When I cannot sleep I enter my sanctuary of prayer and talk with God just as I talk to my husband and just like I communicate with friends. This pleases God, because he loves his child—he IS my father.

"The Lord hates the gifts of the wicked, but delights in the prayers of his people."[3]

I like to delight Him and to honor God by obeying the word.

How do we honor God?

"To do right honors God; to sin is to despise him."[4]

My prayer time is my water of life—during this quiet time with God, I draw my strength. I knit my heavenly, woolen throw and I cover myself when the cold, stormy events fall across my path—they come to us all. As the poem that I used to teach stated—"some days must be dark and dreary." I do not remember who penned the lines, but they are etched in my memory.

At times living contains shockers. On one occasion, my husband and I had driven about a thousand miles on our trip and were within ten miles of our destination. We were cruising in the left land on the expressway at the legal speed limit when an object hit the front windshield on the driver's side.

After the initial shock, we realized that a section of a tire had hit us after the car in front of us had a blow out. We saw the car pull off the pavement and stop.

Sometimes life gives us a slap in the face—a shock which tears the calm pieces of our lives into threads, and we no longer have the emotional energy to pick up the pieces. We need help from a higher source.

That day no damage came to our car; the windshield stood the test just like Christ who is our security, our shelter from the storms, our strong and mighty tower, and our shepherd—our windshield protecting us from all the bugs.

How do we acquire the strong Christian windshield, an armor to protect us? We pray for Him to fit this armor to our human bodies. The Bible tells us to wear the full armor of God to protect us. We can ask for things that are in line with the Holy Spirit's desire for us.

When I was touring a prison cell in Jerusalem wherein Caiaphas was judge, the guide explained that he had been told that so many people were beaten and had leaned against the wall while sitting on the stone floor of the prison that their blood permanently stained the stone walls that we viewed. Sure enough, the walls from the floor to the height of a man's shoulders appeared to be a tea-stained color while the rest of the area above was gray.

Paul knew about this suffering, because he was chained and in prison when he wrote about Jesus in the New Testament. Paul paid a high price for his loyalty to the King of Kings and Lord of Lords, and as I walked out of the prison and up the stone steps, it was with awe I thought I might be walking in the same steps that Jesus walked while he was on earth. It made me feel so unworthy of his blessings and his protection.

My path never crossed with Paul, but he had a strong effect on my life from the words I read that he wrote.

An angel of the Lord crossed the path of shepherds that night and told them that a Saviour had been born in the city of David and that His name was Christ the Lord.[5]

My path never paralleled or crossed the path of these shepherds—indeed could not, but that story has a strong effect on me every Christmas as I read the book of Luke.

Peter passed the path of Jesus and was changed. My path never crossed Peter's, but how I was affected by what I read about him.

I considered how my life today might parallel the life of Zechariah—were there areas in my life that God could address as I read that book? Through the Holy Spirit the word of God is illuminated and facts about our Almighty God reign even in today's society.

Zechariah the prophet saw eight visions in the first six chapters, and later received key commands from God. How could I apply these to my own life? I could use key phrases from this messianic book that reveal fulfilled prophecies of Jesus when I speak to unbelievers and try to give them hope for their future. My life also should radiate the presence of God and should draw others to seek a walk with my heavenly father.[6]

That Jesus is sovereign and reigns over our lives should be evident to people around us. They are waiting to see what our lives portray—an example of good deeds or bad.

In Jericho I stood where the walls of Jericho once guarded the city. Here blind Bartimaeus' path crossed the path of Jesus and what a difference it made in his life! This blind man walked home seeing clearly the path that he should take for the rest of his life.[7]

I thought about the city that I lived in—Memphis—and about what had been written about my city: "Sin got pretty bad in Memphis in 1906. It got so bad that a black minister told of the devil leaving hell on a vacation in which he 'stopped over at Memphis, sat down on Beale Street and rewrote the Ten Commandments, leaving the NOT out of each commandment,'..."[8]

Ballots were rigged, saloons ran day and night, and big gambling establishments flourished in Memphis at that time. Cocaine could be purchased in drug stores and was used by prostitutes for pain for tuberculosis to get them through long nights of suffering.

As a school principal in Memphis, I thought that the use of cocaine was a thing of the 60's and 70's. I did not realize how wrong I was until I read more of Memphis history; I was saddened by the realization that it existed here long before 1906.

In my capacity as a principal, I came into contact with administrators who ruled in love, as well as those who ruled with fear. Some people rule by anger. My brother-in-law cited an example that occurred at Chickasaw Country Club. A man asked him if he could change a twenty-dollar bill. When he replied with the old saying, "I can change it from your hand to mine." The individual became irate! My brother-in-law stated, "I'll never tease him any more."

Some people just enjoy staying in a state of madness. It flavors their negative dispositions. Gentleness and love seemed to have escaped their nature. Goodness is out of character. They even rule their families with anger, but unhappy people need God's love. It is sad to live a lifetime without finding the path to God's love and forgiveness.

Families become divided by hate.

Families are divided by alcohol. An addiction to strong drink can lead to automobile wrecks. I saw on the evening news where a young girl was sentenced in Memphis to twenty-two years in prison for running over two elementary students on the way home from school. She was under the influence of liquor and did not plan to kill the young elementary students, but she was not in control of her reflexes. She had taken the wrong path that day; therefore, her path today was announced by a judge—the path to prison. She had followed a "dark and evil path."[9]

Sometimes the sway of traffic on the expressway almost lulls us to sleep as we drive. Miles and miles of pavement stretch out north and south from Lake City, Florida, to Naples. Around Tampa the noise of six lanes of traffic zoom down the pavement at 70 mph. The rhythm goes faster and faster. I wondered as I drove that day if drugs get people in the same fast rhythm—a little today and more and more tomorrow and the next day.

On *60 Minutes* a professional football player, Lawrence Taylor, was interviewed. He stated that drugs had taken over his life and that he was on drugs the night that his jersey was retired. Crack was the only bright spot in his future after his retirement—the only thing he lived for—he placed them ahead of his children, his wife, or his family. He was totally honest about how drugs had taken over his life.

Drugs demand a faster merry-go-round—a different pace of living. Youth are gradually lulled into sin's rhythm of deception. There is a thrill in being high, peers tell them. Try it; don't be square! Sellers wishing to become rich give them the same sales talk, but what does the Bible say about monies from ill-gotten gains and profits?

"Some men enjoy cheating, but the cake they buy with such ill-gotten gain will turn to gravel in their mouths."[10]

"A fortune can be made from cheating, but there is a curse that goes with it."[11]

We are an impatient society—we demand instant money, instant promotions, instant mashed potatoes, instant French fries, instant coffee, instant tea, and instant pop tarts. All of our electrical machinery in the house gives us more time in our daily schedule, but is this true? Where is that extra time?

I thought about the deer that bounded one night into my path on the highway. Sometime sin blinds us to the real, present danger. That night my mother was in the back seat of my car lying down. I was taking her home from the hospital in Memphis, a hundred-mile trip one way.

It was dark.

I was entering a curve in the road east of Ramer, Tennessee, when my headlights flashed on a deer on the left side of the road. He was stationary. *Stay there; do not move* I thought to myself.

The deer seemed to be drawn to my headlights. He bounded forward and hit the left side of the car and flipped into the air. In the darkness I could no longer see this sleek, antlered deer.

At times we rush headlong into the darkness of sinful activities and into problems created by sin, and we feel the painful results of our actions.

In Memphis there is a building called the Women's Exchange. I go there to eat occasionally with my friends for two reasons: the food is fresh and delicious and they have a great section of gift items to buy. I can browse after I eat and look at handcrafts, baby blankets, or just cute odds and ends.

In Florida, there is a place called Second Time Around where in exchange for a small sum of money you can buy used items, tools, books, furniture, and clothes. It is similar to Goodwill stores and to the Salvation Army store. What some people tire of others need and enjoy.

exchange! A man named Mark heard these words straight from a man's lips, and I am sure he pondered them just as men throughout the century have pondered and puzzled them.

"What shall a man give in exchange for his soul?"[12]

I have heard that women sell their bodies for money. People sell their soul for drugs and alcohol. In my opinion, they sell themselves too cheaply. I am convinced that they are worth much more.

I heard on the news recently that a couple paid $5,000 for a baby. Evidently these people valued one small soul as being worth the price.

What is your soul worth?

In your private devotional time this week, read the following verses to build your faith and strengthen you to take the right path and to make the correct decisions for the next seven days.

Psalm 27:11 • Psalm 28:8 • Psalm 25:8 • Psalm 25:10
Psalm 25:13 • Psalm 25:21

Time with the Master

- Does sin have you blinded like the deer?

- Does any addiction have you in its clutch?

- Do you know the way to escape?

- Is money your God?

- Are you placing anything before Christ?

    Remember He is a jealous God who will have nothing placed before Him.

IF YOU WOULD LIKE, PRAY THIS WITH ME.

Heavenly Father, help me when I am blinded by sin and too weak to say no. Show me a way to escape. I desire your love and guidance. Paths that are wrong for me to take, place those paths behind my back so that I shall not even see them, and lead me in the paths of righteousness for your name's sake. I thank you because you have heard my prayer and I know the answer is on the way. Amen.

23

A Serpentine Path

The weather had mitigated after rays of golden sunshine bathed the farmlands of Tennessee. I was seven years old and eager to explore my grandfather's farm as I ran at full speed down the path toward the watermelon patch where melons were growing larger and larger each week.

Beyond lay a wooded area flanked by the river flowing in a southwestern direction. I enjoyed listening to the gurgling small rills and brooks, but deep waters were not as inviting.

The grapevine hanging wide and inviting was scary, because the water underneath was black and mucky. I could tell that the water was deep, and I did not trust the vine to carry my weight. What if it should break? I could not swim.

I ran down the path adjacent to the river and took the next bank of dirt almost faster than my legs would carry me. But with effort, I kept my balance. I was agile, strong, and fast—faster than any of my classmates, boys or girls. I like to run and broad jump; therefore, I spent many hours entertaining myself with this pastime, but my goal

PATHS THAT CROSS

was to find a ripe watermelon. I enjoyed them better
  straight from the melon patch.

The trail I followed that day was a serpentine, winding path with rotten tree limbs scattered across the dirt walkway. Maybe your life has disappointed you and you think that the winding path is spiraling out of control. Remember these words.

"For the Lord sees clearly what a man does, examining every path he takes.[1]

Satan may be trying to occupy you with your past mistakes like in the book The Screwtape Letters by C. S. Lewis. Satan tells the demons to keep men occupied with their past mistakes—keep them on a path of guilt; if they do this Satan will win their souls.

"But do remember, the only thing that matters is the extent to which you separate the man from the Enemy. It does not matter how small the sins are provided that their cumulative effect is to edge the man away from the Light and out into the Nothing."[2]

He goes on to say "Indeed the safest road to Hell is the gradual one—the gentle slope, soft underfoot, without sudden turnings, without milestones, without signposts."[3]

I have a suggestion for you to follow if one sin that you committed still plagues your mind. When you ask God to forgive you state the exact time and date that you want to be forgiven. For example: On October 5, 2005, please forgive me for _____. You fill in the blank. This really works. I tried it myself.

My sister and I did everything within our power for our mother when she was in the nursing home, but I still wondered if I had done enough. I stayed with her in the hospital following a broken hip; twice I took her to doctor's in Jackson and to a hospital in Memphis, but I was not in the same town with her. My sister who lived about five blocks away visited her six days a week, but that didn't placate me. I knew the things I did far exceeded what I saw others do. I still beat myself up with the thought—did I do everything I could have done while she was alive?

The Serpentine Path

So I talked with God. Lord, you know all the visits I made, all the doctors that I talked with on her behalf, every staff member I contacted—everything I did. I can't continue allowing this question to keep entering my mind. It bothers me, so please forgive my humanity. I think that I showed her my great love and took every step I knew to take, but if I didn't, please forgive me on _____ (and I stated the exact date).

Now, when Satan throws that in my face, I tell him that the matter has been settled in heaven.

* * * *

I followed two serpentine paths this year—one at the airport and one in the Everglades.

"Pull your shoes off; take off your belts with large buckles, and take all you coins out of your pockets," blared the loud announcement made by the short, heavy woman dressed in a navy blue uniform. At the airport, I was in a line that weaved around in five curves which gradually arrived at the security checkpoint.

One distraught mother was giving a tongue lashing to her agitated child in a stroller being teased by an older sibling. We weaved around up and down until we reached the conveyor belt. I placed my shoes, purse, and carry-on luggage on the moving belt to be inspected. The sign that I read stated that there was no need to take off our coats, so I left my jacket on.

"Take off you jacket; it has a metal zipper," stated the official behind the moving belt.

"My vest also has a zipper," I replied. "Should I take it off?"

"No need; it's only plastic."

Boy, he is well trained. I had never noticed the difference between the two zippers on my identical blue nautical outfit.

Sometimes motives are like those two zippers. Some people give presents with an ulterior motive—they desire something in return. This type of person butters up his boss at work to obtain a promotion. Others assist with a pure heart.

Mankind has no radar system that searches the heart.

About that time as I was seated in the airport, I heard a funny, piercing sound that could not be a baby crying. I watched as an older, white-headed lady placed a black case in the arms of another woman. Both were trying to comfort a terrified cat who continued to make the loud, shrill sound.

The ladies were upset.

The black cat was terrified.

Bystanders were staring in disbelief as the commotion continued.

Five minutes passed with the cat's high-pitched vocal screams continuing, until finally, the woman boarded the plane with her black case. I was glad that my flight left later.

There are times when our journey is like that plane ride for the cat—it is frightening. We do not know what is around the next curve in the road. We sense that a whirlwind is spiraling around us and soon we will be caught up in the air and hurled against a building. We are fearful of the consequences of the actions of others outside our control.

"So take a new grip with your tired hands and stand firm on your shaky legs. Mark out a straight path for you feet. Then those who follow you, though they are weak and lame, will not stumble and fall but will become strong."[4]

"Get rid of all bitterness, rage, anger, harsh words, and slander, as well as all types of malicious behavior. Instead, be kind to each other, tenderhearted, forgiving one another, just as God through Christ has forgiven you."[5]

Remember these verses because the Bible says that laughter is healthy for the human body. A jolly heart is like a medicine. It is like sprinkling the right seasoning in a soup.

Time with the Master

- What kind of serpentine path do you think that you are on today?

- What sounds are getting your attention?

- What really bothers you?

- Will you try to trust the two Bible sections quoted previously?

PRAY WITH ME:

Lord, my life seems to be spiraling out of control. Will you take control and place more faith in my heart for trusting you? Thank you for your love and protection. Place your hand of protection around my family and lead us gently into a closer relationship with each other and with you. Thank you that the answer to this prayer is on the way. Amen.

24

GUIDEPOSTS ON THE PATH WITH GOD

The Lord "causes me to stay on a straight path, a narrow, grooved trail of right rather than wrong, obedience rather than rebellion, service rather than self-absorption, discipline rather than impulse, and cross-bearing rather than indulgence."[1]

He lets us rest, He feeds us, then He leads us on this journey up hills, down valleys, and around dangerous curves in the road. When we have a heart to help others—to be of service; when we are fearful, He comforts and keeps us close.

The straightest road I know is across Alligator Alley as it slices the Everglades from Naples to Miami. I have traveled it many times and the sameness in scenery adds no spice to life. It is a different story at the southern end of the West Coast of Florida, 35 miles south of Naples; here lies Everglades City on State Road 29.

You can buy a ticket and ride an airboat which takes you on a meandering trip through miles of grasslands and mangroves via water. A native guide will point out the alligators and wild life indigenous to this area while you can watch for manatees and dolphins.

Virgil, Judy, Drexel and I paid for our tickets. We were ready to view the scenery in the everglades.

After riding for miles in the airboat, I saw one hungry, friendly pelican which landed on our boat and eyeballed my husband who was nearest.

All those meandering, curving turns on this path through the everglades and only one pelican was viewed. Sometimes our search through life for meaning has been similar to the airboat ride—futile until suddenly, with God's help we see the big picture and life has purpose and meaning.

On a boat ride that I took with my son—two dolphins were playing with each other and jumping out of the clear blue waters on the coast near Ft. Myers. I saw more that day without spending a dime—when I was not expecting it than I did the day that I rode for miles in the canals of the everglades.

The unexpected happened and brought with it joy.

Today we have major means of transportation, but I thought of how Thomas Edison had to travel by boat to get to this region. All the lumber for his home had to be transported by boat, but today with all our modes of transportation and all our knowledge, we are still searching for truths, for peace, and for happiness.

The search for the right paths is still man's major concern.

I attended Vanderbilt and the University of Memphis searching for knowledge. I memorized many facts for the tests that I took. I listened to my professors in order to achieve passing grades, but I discovered that the greatest book was one I took with me to college—the Bible. It helped me more to this day than all the plays I studied by Shakespeare, all the novels I took tests on, and all the poetry that I enjoyed reading. I still have these books and I still enjoy them, but I read more from the book I bought as a teenager.

The truths in that book have gone with me and soaked into the fiber of my being. They have gone with me through a thirty-year career in the field of education. These truths have eased the way through many deep ravines and through many difficult periods. They have sustained me every day of my life.

I was reminded of a day when the world was white around me—snow had forced the closing of schools and the governmental offices were also forced to remain closed for the day. After seeing the list of school closing on television, I flipped to channel ten and saw that *Mister Rogers' Neighborhood* was showing the process of making ribbon from plastic pellets. A lot of heat was involved before the ribbon was transferred to small spools ready for the customer to purchase in the store.

After the extreme heat, it was perfect for use! Isn't that just like our lives—sometimes we must go through the fiery trials in order for us to become a more usable Christian vessel for God to use.

"Do not be surprised, dear friends, at the fiery test that is coming upon you, as if you were experiencing something unheard of. Instead, be joyful that you are sharing to some degree the sufferings of Christ, in order that at the revealing of His glory you may be full of Him."[2]

This is how Peter explained hard trials. "So if you are suffering according to God's will, keep on doing what is right and trust yourself to the God who made you, for he will never fail you.[3]

Again I call your attention to the words of Peter, a man who knew about suffering.

"After you have suffered a little while, our God, who is full of kindness through Christ, will give you his eternal glory. He personally will come and pick you up, and set you firmly in place, and make you stronger than ever."[4]

"Do you want more and more of God's kindness and peace? Then learn to know him better and better. For as you better, he will give you, through his great power, everything you need for living a truly good life: he even shares his own glory and his own goodness with us![5]

Then what does Peter say will happen to us as Christians when we learn to know God better and when we realize what he wants us to do?

"God will open wide the gates of heaven for you to enter into the eternal kingdom of our Lord and Savior Jesus Christ."[6]

Today we can work to do the same thing it speaks of in Isaiah—we can be "The repairer of the breach, the restorer of paths to dwell in."[7]

Moses spoke to the children of Israel in what is now Jordan today. These were his words to them. "I call heaven and earth to witness against you that today I have set before you life or death, blessing and cursing. Oh, that you would choose life; that you and your children might live! Choose to love the Lord your God and to obey him and to cling to him, for he is your life and the length of your days."[8]

The last message from Jesus in the last book of the Bible must be very important.

"Behold, I come quickly."[9]

"I am the root and the offspring of David, and the bright and morning star."[10]

"Surely I come quickly."[11]

Today, you can make a choice!

Will you follow the path that God planned for you?

Time with the Master

- Today you must make a choice to continue to follow God or to continue to follow Satan's path. Which choice will you make?

- You have made many choices in your life. Perhaps you have already chosen a mate for life, a career path, a house to buy, etc.

TODAY CHOOSE ETERNAL LIFE AND PRAY WITH ME THIS PRAYER:

Heavenly father, please forgive me for my sins. Grant me mercy. Protect me from Satan's ploys. Place your protection around my family and help me to be the example that I long to be. Lord you are worthy of glory, honor, and praise. In the precious name of Jesus—a name above all other names. Amen.

25

An Unwelcome Path

My emotions were spinning like a spinning wheel—no, I really felt like I was in the center of a hurricane, or maybe my heart was crushed. My sane, methodically arranged life was circling out of orbit. I had no control.

I was seated in the doctor's office with my husband when we heard words that I had not expected. Instead the doctor entered the examination room and calmly stated, "Drexel, the bottom line is you have prostate cancer; the first twelve needles were clear, but the last one, number thirteen, was positive for cancer."

It is hard to describe my emotions at that point. I had really expected the prostate biopsy to come back negative even though his PSA count had been progressively rising to 9.3.

My husband made it clear to me that he wanted our son to be first to hear the bad news. I shall never forget the date: November 19, 2004.

Our son Barry made the airline reservations for us to fly to Ft. Myers, Florida, for the week of Thanksgiving. We shared that the doctor in Memphis stated that his prostate cancer could be treated by surgery or by injecting seeds.

Without our knowledge, God's hand was already at work on a different treatment.

One of Barry's neighbors had a father who was treated at Loma Linda Medical Center in California, for the same reason. My husband contacted him by e-mail and by telephone and received the proper person to communicate with at the hospital. Drexel was instructed to FAX all his reports to them for reviewing.

We spent Christmas in Germantown and after reviewing his case, an appointment was scheduled for February 10-11, 2005.

On January 10, we returned to Florida to spend a month in the sunshine where temperatures rose to 80 degrees during the day. There was no sunshine in my heart—just clouds all around my heart. The days were long even though we were spending quality time with our son, my college roommate, Judy, and her husband Virgil Crowder. Virgil is a big University of Tennessee football fan and a past District Governor for Rotary International. They are so "young at heart" and fun to be around. Besides, my love for Judy was bonded the first day I saw her when I was seventeen years old and a college freshman in Nashville, Tennessee—at dear ole' Peabody at Vanderbilt University.

Drexel is a very private person who worked as a hospital administrator for thirty-five years before retiring, so he asked me not to tell anybody until he made a decision on the type of treatment.

I honored his simple request.

But it was hard for me because I wanted everybody praying for my husband.

On February 9, 2005, we flew from Ft. Myers, Florida, to Ontario, California, and rented a car for the short twenty-five-minute trip to Loma Linda. The next day he was interviewed, more tests were completed, and an appointment was scheduled for 2:00 p.m. so that a pod could be made for

An Unwelcome Path

his Proton Treatment.

Drexel met and talked with about 30 other people who were scheduled for the same proton treatment—all at various stages. He communicated with people who had completed the treatment, years earlier. He also met a man who had prostate surgery eight years before, but the cancer had returned. Today his choice of treatment was to use the Proton Radiation Therapy.

There are options available for people with prostate cancer that we did not know existed before our son's research.

We are thankful that God was already lighting a path for us to follow. At this time, Drexel's forty-four treatments start on February 22, 2005, and we have rented a corporate apartment with all cooking utilities, sheets, towels included—we have a laundry room at our disposal as well as a workout room for exercising.

Now that we are physically prepared, Drexel shared his news with his four brothers and sisters on February 12, 2005. I also told my sister Verlene—my prayer warrior.

I know that this unwelcome path that we are following will help someone along his journey and battle with cancer in the future.

My husband asked me to share this rough path so that the road will not be as rugged for the next men who receive the same diagnosis—cancer.

THE LIGHT AT THE END OF THE ROAD IS GOD'S LIGHT. HE IS THE LIGHT OF THE WORLD. He is always with us lighting our paths. He takes our fears and replaces them with love, joy, peace, fruits of the spirit, and His mercy is renewed for us each morning.

About the Author

Betty Rich Hendon is a 2004 Honoree in *Two Thousand Notable American Women* for her outstanding professional achievements and contributions to society. She is a school board member and is listed in *The World Who's Who Of Women; Most Admired Men And Women Of The Year, 1996; Woman Of The Year; Great Women Of The 21st Century, 2005*; et al.

Her passion is motivating individuals to live a richer, fuller life in tune with God's will.

CONTACT THE AUTHOR

Betty Hendon
1605 N. Germantown Pkwy. Suite 111
Cordova, TN 38018
www.bettyhendon.com
brhendon@midsouth.rr.com

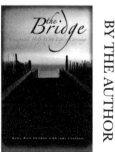

BY THE AUTHOR

The Bridge: Unexpected Help with Life's Crossings.
ISBN 1-932307-08-7

Bible Translations

All scripture references are from the King James Version of the Bible, unless otherwise noted.

Other translations used were the following:

NKJV	New King James Version
	Nashville: Thomas Nelson (1982)
NLT	Holy Bible New Living Translation
	Wheaton: Tyndale House (1996)

The following translations were taken from:

    The Layman's Parallel Bible
    Grand Rapids: Zondervan (1973)

LB	Living Bible
MLB	Modern Language Bible
RSV	Revised Standard Version

Endnotes

CHAPTER THREE

1. *Clark*: Harry H. Clark, *Major American Poets* (New York: American Book Company 1936), 682
2. Psalm 32:8

CHAPTER FOUR

1. Proverbs 22:17-19 (LB)
2. Proverbs 22:4 (LB)
3. Proverbs 22:1 (LB)
4. Proverbs 22:6 (LB)

CHAPTER FIVE

1. *Astoria*: Dorothy Astoria, *The Name Book* (Minneapolis: Bethany House Publishers 1997), 153
2. Ibid., 96

CHAPTER SIX

1. Acts 18:9-10 (LB)
2. John 11:21-33 (LB)
3. Exodus 2 (LB)
4. Psalm 25:10 (LB)
5. Jeremiah 10:23-24a (LB)
6. Jeremiah 29:11-13 (LB)

CHAPTER SEVEN

1. Psalm 32:8 (LB)
2. Psalm 1:1 (MLB)
3. Psalm 1:6 (LB)
4. Psalm 37:34 (LB)
5. Lifetime Original TV, May 22, 2003, "Women Changing the World"

CHAPTER EIGHT

1. John 8:12 (LB)
2. Luke 23:1
3. Luke 23:7
4. Luke 23:11
5. Luke 23:26
6. Luke 23:33, 53
7. Proverbs 20:24(LB)

CHAPTER NINE

1. Proverbs 11:3 (LB)

CHAPTER TEN

1. II Corinthians 10:4
2. II Corinthians 10:4-5 (LB)
3. II Corinthians 6:7
4. Isaiah 51:15 (LB)
5. Romans 8:38-39

Endnotes

6. II Corinthians 4:7(LB)
7. Philippians 4:6-7 (LB)
8. Psalm 91:4
9. I Chronicles 29:12
10. I Chronicles 29:12 (LB)

CHAPTER ELEVEN

1. Appomattox Court House, Division of Publications National Handbook 109, (Washington: U. S. Department of the Interior, Appomattox Court House National Historical Park, Virginia 1980), 57
2. Ibid.
3. Ibid.
4. Psalm 4:8 (NKJV)
5. Psalm 9:15 (NKJV)
6. Joel 3:10
7. Graham: Billy Graham article "Leave Prison by a Different Path," (Memphis: The Commercial Appeal Newspaper, Friday, October 25, 2002), section E4
8. Psalm 1:6 (LB)

CHAPTER TWELVE

1. Proverbs 16:17 (LB)
2. Proverbs 12:25 (LB)
3. Proverbs 12:22 (LB)
4. Philippians 4:8

5. Proverbs 27:17
6. Proverbs 27:19

CHAPTER THIRTEEN
1. Proverbs 30:5 (LB)
2. Psalm 91:1-5 (LB)

CHAPTER FOURTEEN
1. Romans 11:33
2. Proverbs 15:33
3. Proverbs 16:1
4. Proverbs 16:2a
5. Proverbs 16:2b
6. Proverbs 15:14
7. Proverbs 21:11b
8. Proverbs 22:3
9. Psalm 18:36
10. Proverbs 4:14
11. Psalm 37:34

CHAPTER SIXTEEN
1. Psalm 26:11 (LB)
2. Hebrews 13:8 (LB)
3. Hebrews 13:9 (LB)
4. Hebrews 13:15 (LB)

Endnotes

CHAPTER SEVENTEEN
1. Jeremiah 10:23
2. Kay: Andrea Kay article "Each Rung in Career Ladder is Learning Tool," News-Press (Ft. Myers: The News-Press Monday, June 9, 2003), 6
3. Proverbs 3:6

CHAPTER EIGHTEEN
1. Isaiah 59:7b (LB)
2. Isaiah 59:9 (LB)
3. Proverbs 15:15 (LB)
4. Psalm 91:4-6 (LB)
5. *Magness*: Perre MacFarland Magness, *In the Shadows of the Elms* (Memphis: Elmwood Cemetery 2001), 104
6. *Cash*: Billie Cash, *Light Breaking Through* (Greenville:Ambassador Emerald 2003), 131-2
7. Romans 3:3 (LB)
8. Magness, op. cit., 42

CHAPTER NINETEEN
1. Proverbs 22:28 (LB)
2. *LaHaye*: Tim LaHaye and Thomas *Ice, Charting the End Times* (Oregon: Harvest House 2002), 52
3. *Shanks*: Hershel Shanks and Ben *Witherington* III, *The Brother of Jesus* (New York: Harper Collins 2003), 3
4. Proverbs 2:13

5. *Lucado*: Max Lucado, article "Learning to Love." (Minneapolis: Billy Graham Evangelistic Association, Decision Magazine, Volume 44, Number 2, February 2003), 16-19
6. *Magness*, op. cit., 264-265
7. Better Homes and Gardens, February 2003, Volume 81, Number 2, 28-30
8. Isaiah 57:1b
9. Psalm 119:64 (LB)
10. Psalm 119:105 (LB)

CHAPTER TWENTY

1. Civil War Times, Vol. XLI Number 5, October 2002, 50
2. Ibid., 56
3. Proverbs 3:16-23 (LB)
4. *George*: Elizabeth George, *The Lord Is My Shepherd* (Oregon: Harvest House 2002), 12
5. Ibid.
6. *Cash*: Billie Cash with Judy Chatham, *Windows of Assurance* (Greenville: Ambassador Emerald 2001), 193
7. Psalm 37:6
8. Proverbs 23:19 (LB)
9. Proverbs 24:5 (LB)
10. Proverbs 24:13-14 (LB)
11. Isaiah 48:17 (LB)
12. Proverbs 8:2 (NKJV)

Endnotes

CHAPTER TWENTY-ONE
1. Revelation 21:23
2. Hebrews 12:1 (LB)

CHAPTER TWENTY-TWO
1. *Cowman*: Mrs. Charles E. Cowman, *Streams in the Desert* (Michigan: Zondervan 1974), 69
2. Ibid., 283
3. Proverbs 15:8
4. Proverbs 14:2 (LB)
5. Luke 2:11
6. Scalise: Pamela J. Scalise, article "Prisoners of Hope" Decision Magazine (Minneapolis: Billy Graham Evangelistic Association November, 2002), 36-39
7. Mark 10:46-52
8. *Coppock*: Paul R. Coppock, *Memphis Memoirs* (Memphis: Memphis State University Press 1980), 101
9. Proverbs 2:13 (LB)
10. Proverbs 20:17 (LB)
11. Proverbs 20:21 (LB)
12. Mark 8:37

CHAPTER TWENTY-THREE
1. Proverbs 5:21 (NLT)
2. *Lewis*: C. S. Lewis, *Screwtape Letters* (Ohio: Barbour & Company MCMLXXXV), 51
3. Ibid.

4. Hebrews 12:12-13 (NLT)

5. Ephesians 4:31-32 (NLT)

CHAPTER TWENTY-FOUR

1. *Wood*: George O. Wood, *A Psalm in Your Heart* (Springfield: Gospel Publishing House 1997), 94

2. I Peter 4:12-13 (MLB)

3. I Peter 4:19 (LB)

4. I Peter 5:10 (LB)

5. 2 Peter 1:2-3 (LB)

6. 2 Peter 1:11 (LB)

7. Isaiah 58:12b

8. Deuteronomy 30:19-20 (LB)

9. Revelation 22:7

10. Revelation 22:16

11. Revelation 22:20